Broken

Broken

DESIGNING CAREERS IN A FLAWED AND OUTDATED SYSTEM

MARGARET WENIGER

Book Cover by Sheila Maithel • Interior Design by Zoe Norvell
Editing by Carmen Smith

First edition 2026

To my amazing husband and partner Luke, my best friend Chandra, and the world's greatest coach Amy K. This work is a reflection of your belief in me. Your love, guidance, and unwavering support made this book possible. I am endlessly grateful to walk this path with such an extraordinary circle around me.

Table of Contents

PREFACE

A Love Letter

My obsession began after I was fired for a third time since becoming a mom.

It was January 2021, and I was at the end of my rope emotionally and mentally, feeling like I had no options. How did this happen? How had things gotten this bad?

I had spent the last twelve years intentionally building a career in tech sales leadership, defying the odds as a woman in a male dominated field. Each step of the way, I took time to reflect on what I liked and disliked, which environments were a good fit and which were not, and consulted mentors on big decisions. I took pride in being self-aware enough to recognize when to walk away from opportunities. I had rapidly ascended in my career and the pinnacle of success felt within reach. I had done everything right, or so I thought.

The non-LinkedIn version of my twelve-year career went like this: I had been fired twice after having babies, laid off once, and forced to resign from not just one but two jobs I loved. On paper it sounds pretty grim. And it was. After all that happened, I was no longer proud of what I'd accomplished. I was ashamed. I was convinced I was broken. "Something must be wrong with me," I thought.

Desperate to understand where I'd gone wrong, I began interviewing women about the stories behind their careers. I spoke with over a hundred women of all ages across nine countries and countless industries. What I learned shocked me.

Through the process of these interviews, I stumbled upon a shared experience. Of these women, 78% had made at least one major career change. Each of them shared some version of feeling that their experience was "odd" or "unusual" or "unconventional." They also seemed to be working from the same secret playbook to help them navigate changes in their careers.

I realized that, although the details of my story were different, my journey wasn't unique. This path of pivoting careers was one many women had walked before. I found myself wondering, "If career change is so normal, why does everyone think they're alone in this experience? How could such extraordinary women believe they're broken? If this self-doubt is so prevalent, how many other ambitious women have experienced the same thing?"

This discovery was so much bigger than me and my individual journey. With renewed passion, I set out with a lofty ambition: I would create something to ensure no other ambitious woman would ever have to feel broken, alone, or unsure what to do when she faced a crossroad in her career. She would not fear the voice telling her there was more; instead, she would feel empowered to explore who she was becoming.

For the next two years, I poured everything into understanding how we had gotten here. How it was that brilliant women found themselves filled with shame, fear, or doubt about wanting to change careers or traveling an unconventional path. How we were so convinced of our brokenness.

The result of my obsessive search is this book. A love letter to you.

I have put everything I've learned into this book so it can serve as a guide and a source of validation to you as you navigate your career. As you read these pages, my goal is for you to feel seen, understood, and supported. You are no longer alone in this journey; now you have a roadmap. Not a shortcut or a quick fix, but a beginning.

In this book, I'll challenge you to disrupt old narratives and rethink key relationships. Things might get murkier before they get better. But your choice to honor that voice inside you, calling you toward more, is a worthy pursuit. Listening to your voice will create positive ripples beyond what you can imagine.

If you're ready to choose courage and dare to design a career based on what you truly want, then turn the page and let's begin.

1

WHY WE FEEL STUCK

ONE

The Deinstitutionalization of Careers

> "The corporation, under the consultants' helm, was no longer an enduring venture. It became a momentary assemblage of whose value was not in tomorrow's progress but in today's stock price."
>
> — Louis Hyatt

What we're experiencing at work today was set into motion before many of you were even born, let alone thinking about a career. Do you remember those good old days when companies provided internal resources to help us choose career paths that aligned with our skills, then helped us create a plan to achieve those goals and provided training so we were prepared for that next move?

Yeah, me neither. Jack Welch killed that in the 1980s and '90s before millennials, who are now nearly half of full-time employees, ever joined the workforce.

We were handed a career playbook rooted in practices that were already obsolete by the time we joined the workforce. Despite mounting evidence to the contrary, meritocracy—the idea that anyone could move up in the world if they were educated, willing to work hard, and do a great job—remained the prominent PR message. That's what we heard, and that's what we believed.

The reality is that careers were becoming increasingly deinstitutionalized.[i] The institutions that once provided a clear career path from point A to Z no longer existed, a shift driven by three primary drivers:

- Employees were now expenses, not assets
- Company lifespans were shortening
- Technology was accelerating

How Did We Get Here?

Throughout most of the twentieth century it was common for individuals to work at a single company for the entirety of their career. Companies believed they were hiring employees for their career lifetime, and the professional development companies provided to their

---

i In her book "Working Identities", Herminia Ibarra discusses the shift in modern careers away from linear paths, fixed roles, and institutional career growth towards a more fluid work landscape where careers are non-linear and self-directed.

employees mirrored this investment. Throughout their careers, employees might spend up to four years receiving on-the-job training.

Important moves in our careers were institutionalized, and there was a scripted path within a company or profession. Employees might change departments or teams but under the umbrella of the same company. If you wanted to ascend the proverbial ladder, there were clear steps to follow, and you knew how long each step would take.

As a result, new hires fresh out of college were not expected to know exactly what they wanted to do for work. Instead, new employees were encouraged to rotate through various departments to learn multiple aspects of the business, so they had a breadth of experience to pull from as they rose into leadership positions. They were encouraged to "job hop," if you will.

Graduate degrees were seen as nice-to-haves but not required for those who sought to become senior leaders. It was not unusual for companies to provide internal executive programs that could last up to eighteen months. You might be wondering, "How did things become so distorted from this reality in such a short span of time?" Unfortunately, the answer is rather simple: a series of individuals with tremendous power and influence used their platforms for greed rather than the common good.

The Shift

During the Industrial Era, General Electric (GE) became

one the biggest American institutions. The company was founded by Thomas Edison in 1892 when he invented the light bulb. GE continued to develop innovative technology over the years, such as X-ray machines, the first home televisions, commercial jet engines, and nuclear power.

As a steward for American companies, GE prioritized responsibility to one's country and therefore its employees who were citizens of that country. GE viewed their employees as the company's greatest asset, and a primary goal of the company was "maximizing employment security." Profits were poured back into employee programs first, investments in research and innovation second, with the remaining going to shareholders.

For all intents and purposes, it appeared this strategy was highly effective. GE was known for its technological innovation and management best practices. As one of the largest companies in the US, it was often looked to as the blueprint for how other CEOs built and ran their companies.

Then, at the end of the 1960s, the impact of the changing economic driver from manufacturing to information technology was visibly disrupting the business world. Computer systems could now manage, process, protect, and exchange information. The emergence of this new technology also made access to broader markets more feasible, and for the first time, US companies faced global competition.

With the changing economic climate, influential executives like Jack Welch from GE and other executives from

America's largest corporations came together in 1973 to strategize how to operate in this new global market. Together, they formed a lobbying group known as the Business Roundtable, which was built on the theories of leading economist Milton Friedman.

Friedman was a big advocate for free markets, and for minimizing government regulations. His book, *Capitalism and Freedom*, sold over 400,000 copies. Free markets, he argued, would both fix efficiency problems and help nations and individuals in the long run. The priority of a company should no longer be on innovation and employee development; instead, "the responsibility of the business is to promote profitability."

While the series of events and variables influencing this belief were complex, when we strip away the noise we can see this shift for what it was: an extreme pendulum swing in the opposite direction. In one moment, companies prioritized people and innovation over everything; in the next, they prioritized profits at all costs. Both extremes were unsustainable, but unfortunately the Business Roundtable was blind to this and subscribed wholeheartedly to the philosophy that a business' responsibility was to drive profitability above all else. This became the most important role of a corporate executive, all in the name of "helping our nation and individuals."

Inevitably, prioritizing profitability at all costs devolved into driving profitability for shareholders and viewing executives as the key assets for doing so. Over the next forty years, money began flowing toward the top of organizations and away from employees. Since 1978, executive compensation packages have grown to an excessive 940% compared to the meager 12% increase for employees.[1]

This ruthless prioritization of profitability at all costs—a shift that would forever change American businesses—spread like wildfire through the business world, becoming the hallmark of Jack Welch's campaign to become the next CEO of GE.

Profits Over People

A big believer in Friedman's theories, Jack Welch justified his seemingly ruthless management decisions as his moral obligation to be a good steward of the company and ensure profitability for its shareholders. During his twenty-year reign as CEO of GE, Welch was idolized by other CEOs and shareholders for his uncanny ability to hit quarterly and annual projections year after year. He consistently found a way, no matter what it took, to make the numbers work.

Welch would become well-known for leveraging three go-to strategies to ensure the company met shareholder expectations:

1. Layoffs
2. Mergers and acquisitions
3. Rank and yank

Welch first showcased the power of layoffs in 1977, when he was named a frontrunner for the GE CEO position. As a frontrunner, he was put in charge of the appliance division and given the directive to grow the division. The original plan when Welch arrived was to expand the already profitable division. Determined that overseas competition would make it more difficult to continue turning a profit despite expanding the division, Welch instead proposed a significant headcount reduction to increase margins. Leveraging the unknown of shifting markets, Welch convinced GE executives to approve the proposed reduction strategy at one of the largest GE facilities that employed over 23,000 people. GE saw an initial boost in profits after laying off 4,600 factory employees, ultimately rewarding Welch for this strategy by naming him CEO of GE in 1981.[2] Layoffs would become one of Welch's go-to tactics to drive profits.

The Explosion of Inorganic Growth

Needing a way to neutralize the fallout of mass layoffs and constant turnover, Welch recognized an opportunity to grow revenue and acquire innovation through mergers and acquisitions rather than developing it in-house. Not only would this increase his status as the company grew, it would also show revenue growth in the short term.

Touting the success of this strategy would again fundamentally change the face of business in America. In 1978, three years before Welch took over as CEO of GE, there were just 1,615 mergers and acquisitions (M&As). From 1981 to 2001, M&As would grow 1000%, reaching a record high in 2021 at 29,642.[3]

Around the same time Welch was ascending at GE, another set of highly influential men further validated the extreme approach of profits over people. Thomas Peters and Robert Waterman Jr. were McKinsey Directors who studied their consulting clients' management techniques in an attempt to capture what made them the best-managed companies. In 1982, they published *In Search of Excellence*, a book based on their research that provided a new model for how corporations should restructure to compete in the increasingly global economy. "Excellent companies are not really 'long-term thinkers,'" the book touted, and excellent global companies possessed a "simple form, lean staff."

The downside of this strategy was the often overlooked complexity of combining two companies. If you've ever been part of a merger or acquisition, you've likely experienced firsthand the ramifications of joining two sets of cultures, procedures, systems, data, and customer relationships. Too often, the best of the acquired company is slowly stripped away after an acquisition or merger. Those who remain are under pressure to prove they deserved to stay. Entire companies are dismantled and destroyed to temporarily show strong growth numbers, overlooking the customers and employees who suffered in the process.

Despite 70-90% of M&A transactions failing, this strategy has only grown in popularity since its inception in the '80s, especially with the rise of tech startups.[4] Its popularity highlights how deeply entrenched executives have become in prioritizing short-term gains and personal gains over the greater good and long-term stability.

The Super Spreaders

The final strategy Jack Welch became known for was one that had long been practiced by renowned consulting firm, McKinsey & Co. Since consulting wasn't something you could get a degree for at the time, McKinsey recruited MBA graduates fresh out of the Ivys. The logic was that these graduates had instant credibility due to the presumed rigor of an Ivy League education, as well as an exposure to a wide variety of business models and problems using a case study method. They were also young, competitive, and impressionable, which meant could indoctrinate these new employees into their culture and teach them the McKinsey way.

The McKinsey way was one of constant pressure to perform. The firm's philosophy was you are either moving up or out. There was no such thing as a steady state. MBA graduates were hired at ten times the rate of need in anticipation of turnover. In the 1990s, only one in five associates became partners, and just half of partners ever reached a director level, where they would finally be free of constant scrutiny.[5] Work was project-based and performance constantly monitored. This lack of career safety was seen as a core reason for the firm's success. Consultants, including partners, had to produce or risk losing their jobs.

Yet the allure of working for McKinsey did not dwindle from its toxic hustle culture; quite the contrary, it bolstered its attractiveness. McKinsey consultants were well compensated for their work, and the promise of money at the partner level was used as an incentive to keep grinding in the present—even if they got cut in the process. When a consultant was deemed unfit to be a partner, the company framed the decision to let them go as an opportunity, not a failure. These employees received a generous severance package, and placement counselors at McKinsey helped them find good jobs in the hopes that these former consultants would hire the firm in the future and continue spreading the McKinsey way.

The plan was successful. Over the decades, these highly indoctrinated consultants moved into middle and upper management across major US corporations, taking with them the mentality that employee value was tied only to performance, that if you weren't actively moving up you should be moved out. As Louis Hyman put it in his book *Temp: How American Work, American Business, and the American Dream Became Temporary:*

> The influence of consultants was felt not only when they worked for Boston Consulting Group (BCG) or McKinsey - it was felt after they left. This logic, peculiar to this very niche world, would later be projected onto the economy at large. The instability and high pay of the consulting world fed on itself, as the people who believed in this model of management cut the staffs of corporations, and, when that was

> done, joined the staffs. It worked for them. Why would it not work for the rest of America?

Welch, like McKinsey, saw the belief that companies should provide security and stability to their employees as naive and outdated. Fear, he believed, was a far more effective and powerful motivator. When named CEO, Welch deployed his vitality curve across the entire organization—or, as it was more crudely known in the company, the "rank and yank" approach. It was eerily similar to McKinsey's "Up or Out" philosophy.

Leaders at GE were required to stack rank their employees by performance. Even in high-performing teams, managers were forced to name 10% of employees as top performers, 80% as middle, and 10% at the bottom. Even if the entire team had done a great job, those who fell into the bottom 10% were laid off at the end of the year. The message was clear: perform or get out.

Much like "failed" McKinsey consultants, former GE executives were swooped up into middle and upper management positions across America. Companies hired these executives in hopes that they could bring the same success to their struggling organizations. At one point in the early 2000s, five of the top 30 Dow Jones Industrial Average companies were run by CEOs who had formerly worked as executives under Jack Welch. These professionals prioritized short-term thinking, profits at all costs, and "perform or move out" mindsets, which took over corporate America in an alarmingly short span of time.

The Fallout

As Welch's "Campaign Against Loyalty" spread to other major players, and more cutthroat consultants were contracted or hired full-time in key leadership roles, it wasn't long before the fallout from these short-term strategies exposed their long-term consequences. Between 1980 to 1995, the number of Americans working for major corporations who feared layoffs more than doubled, from 14%[6] to 36%[7] As of July 2025 that number has risen to an alarming 70%.[8] The belief that you could work at the same company through retirement was quickly becoming a thing of the past, and employees were facing a new reality: they would have to look elsewhere for career support and growth.

Along with this decline in stability came a decline in employee training. Executives rationalized that it didn't make fiscal sense to invest in individuals who would eventually leave or be let go. This thought process led to a decline in the training budget over the coming decades; today, companies spend a whopping 2% of payroll on training.[9]

In this new landscape, companies were no longer the providers of career training. Instead, the expectation (and burden) fell to employees, who now had to subsidize their own education and skill development if they wanted to progress in their careers.

Economist Louis Hyatt puts it bluntly: "The corporation, under the consultants' helm, was no longer an enduring venture. It became a momentary assemblage whose value was not in tomorrow's progress but in today's stock price." The shock waves from this obsession with short-term gains, with no consideration given to long-term growth, has destabilized corporate institutions and led to a declining lifespan for Fortune 500 companies. In the last twenty years, the average lifespan of S&P 500 companies has declined 40%, from thirty-five years to twenty-one years. McKinsey & Company is forecasting that, by 2027, 75% of companies currently quoted in S&P 500 will have disappeared.[10]

The destabilization of large corporations has been a significant factor in the disappearance of institutional support for career advancement. Professionals can no longer look to their company as a source of guidance; rarely can they even get a timeline for promotions or next steps. When tech startups emerged, some hoped they would bring with them a new work culture. But as these startups rose in power and prominence, it quickly became clear that they were operating under the same Welch playbook, despite leading the way in disruptive technology. In fact, in 2023 alone, the tech industry accounted for over 250,000 of employees impacted by layoffs.[11]

Tech Boom

The 1990s and its dotcom boom gave rise to the glamorous tech startup, where new companies got huge investments and IPOs with little to no product or revenue to show for it. These companies cleverly positioned themselves as anti-convention. Big corporate companies, who had been seen as leaders throughout much of the twentieth century, had become bloated, inefficient, and slow to innovate due to their goliath size; quick changes to adapt to market conditions were nearly impossible. Tech entrepreneurs believed they were leading the way out of this outdated business model. But instead of disrupting the systems that had made these large organizations so dysfunctional, tech founders proved to be their next heir.

Tech founders touted the importance of a return to the customer and a passion for building company cultures where employees could thrive and where innovation reigned supreme. Founders wrapped up this "new" philosophy with alluring employee packages and promises of "making big $" when the company got its big payday. If employees were devoted, if they showed up, if they performed well, they, too, would reap the rewards of the grind.

Much like McKinsey, these tech founders recruited young, smart, inexperienced professionals newly graduated from prestigious universities—impressionable, eager individuals who were ready to make a name for themselves and had few obligations outside of work. They advertised employee perks that appealed to a young demographic, like free lunches, cold brew on tap, kegs in the office, and an open floor plan instead of stuffy offices.[12]

But from another angle, this approach looked all too similar. These companies packaged profitability over personal growth or career advancement by giving its employees things that made it easy to stay at the office, put in the work, and not take breaks. Without the restriction of walls or doors, they could know exactly how much (or how little) their employees were actually working. And by the way, the founders emphasized, without the hard work of every individual, no one would get that big payday. A motivation that smacked of fear, not freedom.

Tech didn't deliver on its promise to innovate a better way of working; rather, it ever so slightly turned the same dysfunctional wheel—steering corporate America in the same direction Welch set decades prior, hiding under a similar guise of progress.

The too often overlooked reality is that working for startups is high risk. Startups with paid employees have less than a 50% survival rate after five years,[13] and they're not immune to acquisitions either. Over the last three decades, the percentage of venture capital-backed startups that were acquired has skyrocketed from roughly 10% to 90%, with around 7% of those acquisitions done purely to squelch emerging competition.[14] In these "killer acquisitions," as researchers have coined them, the competitive projects are shelved and the employees disposed of.

Even if the company is able to survive five years that doesn't mean the employee will. The pace and pressure at these startups is often unsustainable. Companies who describe themselves as innovative have an average tenure of just two years due to the grinding pace they require from their employees. Much like McKinsey, these companies preach a "next person up" mentality for these highly coveted roles: If you don't want to be on our rocketship, we'll find someone else who does.

Market research on the top five US-based tech companies—Google, Microsoft, Salesforce, Amazon, and Apple—showed that between 48-62% of their employees were between the ages of twenty and thirty.[15] Across the board, less than 10% of employees were over the age of forty. The intention at these companies is clear: Bring in young talent, work them hard, and when they burn out, find the next young talent ready to take their spot. Long-term career development is out of the picture entirely.

As corporate America became increasingly volatile, executives doubled down on their belief that shareholders should get top priority rather than recognize the growing issues stemming from such short-term strategies. The fallout of this shortsightedness would land squarely on the shoulders of millennials—a generation who would be gaslighted into believing their struggles meant they lacked grit; in reality, of course, they're experiencing the consequences of something put in motion long before they ever joined the workforce.

The Gaslighting of a Generation

Millennials entered the job market at a critical juncture in the professional landscape. Unbeknownst to millennials, the strategies being preached by their parents, college advisors, mentors, and future employers on how to have a successful career were already outdated. By the time the eldest millennials were entering the workforce in the early 2000s, the short-term strategies deployed by Jack Welch and repackaged by tech startups were beginning to show cracks.

False Guidance #1 - A College Degree Is The Key To Your Career

Between 1969 to 1985, the percentage of students attending college to "become financially well off" rose from 40% to 71%.[16] A four year education not only became more accessible, it also became the default if you wanted a successful career. A longitudinal study of high school students in the late '90s found that more than 70% expected to work in "professional" jobs as doctors, lawyers, professors, and business managers.[17] Except there wasn't enough demand in these professions for the amount of interest. In fact, there were six times the number of students interested in being doctors than the projected positions that would be available when these students would enter the job market.[18]

Getting a college degree was no longer a guarantee to securing a good salary that would help offset the price tag of attending school. As college degrees became more accessible, they were no longer the key differentiator employers used for hiring, and it was becoming increasingly clear that there were no longer any guarantees for a college graduate. But this shift wasn't the only headwind millennials would face entering the job market.

False Guidance #2 - Pick Something and Stick With It

The first decade of millennials entering the workforce brought with it two financial crashes: the dotcom crash of 2000 that would heavily impact the tech industry, and the Global Financial Crisis in 2008—the most significant economic downturn since the Great Depression. Unemployment rates reached as high as 10% in October of 2009.[19] Millennials quickly found themselves facing a massive curveball. Jobs were scarce for everyone, let alone someone just graduating with little or no "real" experience.

Just ask any elder millennial[ii] about the early part of their career and you will hear some version of "Well, I graduated in 2008 and you know how things were going then. There were no jobs or even paid internships in my field and so I…

> **Option 1:** Took whatever work I could find so I could pay down student loans until the job market improved.
>
> **Option 2:** Decided to ride it out and went back to get my master's.
>
> **Option 3:** Took whatever I could, thinking I would eventually get back to my planned career. But I unexpectedly found success and kind of fell backwards into this career.

---

ii Elder Millennials are classified as anyone born between the years 1980-1985

While there were exceptions, this was the shared experience for most college educated millennials. With 62% of millennials saddled with student debt, there was immediate pressure to take a job, any job, that would help them pay off their student loans.[20] Except unemployment rates were so high that experienced talent was on the market and new graduates were finding themselves competing with tenured professionals for the same entry-level positions.

The poor job market and forced career pivots led many millennials to try out careers on the job. Unlike previous generations, however, there were few corporate development programs to facilitate this exploration within a company. In an effort to save money, companies decreased their budget for career development and growth programs; training program investment declined an average of 22% throughout the first decade of the new millennium.[21] On very rare occasions, employees could move within an organization to develop their careers, but most had to change companies altogether if they wanted to pursue any sort of career development.

This behavior led to the ultimate smear campaign by employers looking to deflect attention away from their own greedy practices. Millennials became dubbed the "Job Hopping Generation" and were labelled as disloyal, lazy, and selfish. These were the same companies who removed programs that encouraged employee loyalty and didn't think twice before doing massive rounds of layoffs. Instead of looking at themselves for their high turnover, they blamed this new generation and their unwillingness to work hard. Hiring managers still cite job change as their number one concern when evaluating candidates.

The tragic result of this widespread smear campaign is that 83% of millennials believe changing jobs multiple times will hurt their chances of landing a job in the future.[22] Given this, it's no surprise that we downplay changing careers or even avoid the idea of making a change altogether. There have been real consequences for those choices despite the very logical reasons behind them.

We did not get here overnight. The reality we are operating within was set in motion before you ever started your career. But knowing how we got here is a key piece to understanding how we want to move forward.

TWO

Hustle. Burnout. Recover. Repeat

"Burnout is what happens when you try to avoid being human for too long."

—Emily Nagoski

Angela Duckworth went viral in 2013 after giving a Ted Talk called "Grit: The Power of Passion and Perseverance." In her talk, Duckworth shared groundbreaking research on what differentiated those who succeeded from those who didn't. What had she discovered? Success was not based on talent or IQ but grit, which Duckworth described as "having the passion and perseverance to pursue long-term goals. Being committed to your future, day in and day out. Not for just the week or month but for years."

Fast forward a few years, Duckworth released a book expanding on her research and its broader applications in professional careers. Overnight it became a New York Times bestseller, and leaders across the country bought copies to share with their organizations and teams. This response proved the continued strength of the American Dream in our collective imagination. A person's future, we want to believe, is not determined by where they were born or what schools they attended. Anyone can be successful if they're willing to work really hard, go above and beyond, and stick with things past where others drop out.

Unfortunately, there were some significant issues with Duckworth's book. For starters, the entire premise of grit hinges on an unspoken agreement that the definition of success is mastery in one's field (ex. winning the National Spelling Bee, becoming a professional athlete). This is certainly one definition of success, but Duckworth presented it as the universal definition. Even if we were to presume this was the universal definition of success, the math still isn't mathing. To be the best means you are likely in the top 10% of your field. Which means that for 90% of people, success is unattainable. The subtext of this belief is that failure to achieve this definition of "success" is a failure in something you have control over. Failure to be gritty.

Duckworth goes on to proclaim that "the grittier an individual is, the fewer career changes they're likely to have," revealing Duckworth's own bias regarding linear career paths despite making several career changes of her own, from management consultant to seventh grade teacher to professor and researcher at Wharton.

But these glaring discrepancies were overlooked because the research findings supported what people wanted to believe. If you are part of a marginalized community, of course you want to believe your success is within your control. You just have to be willing to work for it. The ugly side of that message, though, is that any failure you experience on your way to "success"/field mastery is due to an inherent personal deficiency rather than operating in a broken system.

For business executives, *Grit* validated their belief that true A-players should be willing to do whatever it takes to help a company achieve their goals. It emboldened them to demand this level of commitment from their team, and any employee who attempted to set healthy boundaries was deemed as lacking the necessary grittiness to succeed.

The success of *Grit* was yet another demonstration of western cultures' obsession with the extreme. In 2006, economist Sylvia Ann Hewlett studied professionals who were high earning "workaholics" to better understand their attitudes and motivations. Hewlett uncovered that the once sixty hour workweek that led to the top positions had simply become par for the course at any level—with no promise of advancement.

"Our data revealed that 62% of high-earning individuals work more than 50 hours a week, 35% work more than 60 hours a week, and 10% work more than 80 hours a week.[23]" Hewlett also created a subcategory known as "extreme jobs," which painted an even more alarming picture of what corporate America now expected from their employees.

Extreme jobs are ones in which at least five of these elements exist:

- Unpredictable flow of work
- Fast-paced work under tight deadlines
- Inordinate scope of responsibility that amounts to more than one job
- Work-related events outside regular work hours
- Availability to clients 24/7
- Responsibility for profit and loss
- Responsibility for mentoring and recruiting
- Large amount of travel
- Large number of direct reports
- Physical presence at workplace at least ten hours a day

A disturbing 56% of professionals who met the "extreme" classification were working an average of seventy or more hours per week.

Hewlett's research highlighted how America's obsession with extremes was particularly dangerous for individuals who considered themselves to be type A or high achievers. Nearly two-thirds of these individuals believed the pressure and the pace of work they experienced was self-inflicted and a result of their personality type. "Extreme professionals don't feel exploited; they feel exalted."The fact that these individuals were less connected at home, struggled to maintain healthy lifestyles, and often failed to get enough sleep was not viewed with alarm. Instead, they were praised for their grit. By accepting and claiming a true passion for their work, they normalized the dysfunctional relationship embedded in this new career landscape, inadvertently holding up toxic productivity as the standard that everyone should follow. Everyone who wanted to be "successful," that is.

If You Aren't Hustling Are You Even Trying?

Duckworth's *Grit* was simply a period at the end of a sentence that western culture had written long ago. Over the last century, there has been a radical shift from seeing leisure as a status symbol to the glorification of hustle and, on the flipside, viewing rest with utter disdain. It would be difficult to point to any one thing as a root cause of this shift, but there are several factors that have influenced it.

The information era brought with it the development of a knowledge-intensive economy, where office jobs were more highly valued than factory and trade jobs. Employers started using four year degrees as a filter criteria to quickly identify qualified knowledge workers. Because of this, access to a college education meant the opportunity to increase your earning potential and, as a result, your status. This was the promise of the American Dream.

But as college education became more accessible, the American Dream slowly turned into a nightmare. By the end of the twentieth century, nearly 90% of high school seniors expected to attend college. A four year degree was no longer an advantage but table stakes. Since employers could no longer qualify candidates based on whether or not they had degrees, they began tiering out universities and asking for, or in some cases requiring, advanced degrees.

These increased expectations and demands, combined with the belief in meritocracy, wove together a dangerous narrative for the future workforce. Failure to get accepted into top schools meant applicants must have lacked some personal ability. Surely the system itself couldn't be to blame.

According to psychologist Thomas Curran, "Meritocracy falsely and insidiously connects the principles of educational and professional achievement, status, and wealth with innate personal value." In Curran's research on perfectionism, he cautions that "young people are taught that the principles of meritocracy are good, fair, and just. In response, they are compelled to demonstrate their merit, set increasingly higher and unrealistic goals, and come to define themselves in the strict and narrow terms of personal achievement."

After decades of rewarding excessive work and perpetuating the myth of meritocracy, busyness in Western culture has become interchangeable with one's status. The more an individual believes in their social mobility and the promise of the American Dream, the more likely they are to put weight into busyness as a sign of social status.

It should come as no surprise that the pursuit of extremes would eventually hit a breaking point. In 2019, the World Health Organization designated burnout as an occupational phenomenon, but it would take a global pandemic to bring into focus just how extreme and distorted work expectations had become.[24]

I Can't Even Right Now

Although many of you may not need a definition, burnout is a psychological syndrome emerging as a response to chronic interpersonal stressors on the job. There are three key components of burnout:[25]

1. Emotional exhaustion. The fatigue that comes from caring too much, for too long.
2. Depersonalization. The depletion of empathy, caring, and compassion.
3. Decreased sense of accomplishment. An unconquerable sense of futility: feeling that nothing you do makes any difference.

It's important to note that stress is different from stressors. Stressors are what activate the stress response. They can be internal stressors, such as having an inner critic or perfectionism, which has risen over 33% in the United States between 1989 and 2016.[26] They can also be external stressors, such as work demands, money pressures, family relationships, societal norms and expectations, and toxic work environments. Both types of stressors, internal and external, are interpreted by your body as a threat, causing a neurological and physiological response.

In 2022, 43% of professional women reported experiencing unprecedented levels of burnout, nearly 39% higher than their male counterparts.[27] One explanation for this burnout discrepancy is tied back to gender norms, where women are expected to be nurturing, caring, and selfless. These expectations and the imprinting of social norms of what a woman "should" be can lead to compassion fatigue—the cost of caring for others and shouldering their emotional pain.

Compassion fatigue is a primary cause of burnout in professions that are typically dominated by women, such as teaching, social work, and health care. Even in their careers, women are expected to attend to others' needs while dismissing their own stress, which often results from this caretaking. Compassion fatigue symptoms include:

1. Minimizing or dismissing suffering that isn't the most extreme; "Someone else has it worse."
2. Feeling helpless, hopeless, or powerless, while also feeling personally responsible for doing more.
3. Staying in a bad situation out of a sense of grandiosity; "If I don't do it, no one will," or "I can't just leave them."

Just because you can take care of others doesn't mean you should.

Beware of Burnout FOMO

If you're reading this book, I'd be willing to bet that you surround yourself with fellow driven, ambitious women who share your same standards for excellence. Which means that burnout may be a common experience for you, your coworkers, and even your social circle. Burnout might even be a way to connect with your community and provide you with a sense of belonging.

Many of the women I interviewed had a close relationship with burnout. In fact, burnout was a main catalyst for change in their lives. The catalyst often took the form of an event or experience that served as a wake-up call, revealing that pushing herself to the razor's edge of exhaustion was not sustainable. This shift in perspective occurs for each of us for different reasons, whether it is a global pandemic, health issues, becoming a mother, or even the loss of a job. But the hope is that by reading this book you won't need to experience burnout before choosing yourself.

As you begin improving your relationship with burnout, you may notice a shift in the way you engage with those in your circle. It can be tempting to look at friends, family, and colleagues who are always so busy, even on the brink of burnout, and fear that you're missing out (FOMO, in other words). You start thinking, "Why is everyone so busy and I'm not? Should I be doing something? Am I just being lazy? Am I not as important as them?" Your inner critic is panicking because breaking the burnout cycle is unfamiliar territory. It's also a sign of growth. An absence of burnout doesn't mean something is wrong; it's just a signal that you're stretching beyond both your comfort zone and society's. Burnout is still a celebrated syndrome, but remember where those thoughts are coming from and what they actually point to: They are not truths but rather myths perpetuated by the illusion of meritocracy. And they've been in play long before your career began. Tackling burnout is an uphill battle, with corporations and gender expectations at the top.

The Illusive Concept of Work-Life Balance

Arguably one of the most common questions asked of any woman featured on a career-focused panel is, "How do you do it? How do you have it all?" I've heard countless responses to this question, ranging from "you can have it all, just not at the same time" to "you can't." While we'll dig into this topic much deeper in the next section, there are a few pearls of wisdom I've learned from my conversations with successful women about how to think through our own definitions of work-life balance.

1. **It's Fluid.** Holding ourselves to a standard of achieving the perfect work-life balance every day or even every week is aggressive, borderline cruel, and adds undue pressure. Instead, it's important to monitor the natural ebb and flow of our energy and attention levels against the ongoing demands of life. For example, if you have a critical deadline at work, that might mean your career demands more

of your attention than usual. But it has a natural give and take.

2. **It's Highly Personal.** Balance is not about a timesheet that reads 50/50 work/personal. Defining balance is about energy management. It's important to work things into your day and week that are just for you.
3. **It Doesn't Involve Comparisons.** Sometimes the most obvious things trip us up the most. Your situation and circumstances *are* unique (see #2). The only thing that matters when it comes to work-life balance is whether or not *you* feel balanced (and you're honest about this with yourself).
4. **It Changes Over Time.** Life is ever evolving and the demands you face will change depending on what stage of life and career you're in. Give yourself grace. We are all a work in progress. Create space at least twice a year to tune in with yourself and adjust the dials of time and energy allocation as needed.
5. **It Reframes Rest.** The moment you consider giving yourself rest is usually when the inner (and often outer) "shoulds" kick into high gear. If you never give yourself rest, then the best version of you isn't showing up. Would you rather be fully present or give people a shell of yourself?

At the end of the day, hustle culture and burnout are still the norm. Despite more recognition of the ramifications of excessive work and the biological damage associated with burnout, we still operate in a world that will take as much as we will give. A world where companies believe they deserve all of our attention. We cannot control others, much less corporations, but we can make changes to how we show up and navigate our own lives, both professionally and personally. Which is what we'll turn to next.

THREE

When Your Mind Works Against You

"You don't have to believe everything you think."

—Susan David

Until this point in the book, we've primarily looked at the external forces at play within our careers. In this chapter, we're shifting our focus inward. Much like external forces, we have many internal forces that play a big role in our careers. These forces include cognitive biases that keep us stuck and pesky inner critics that love to plant seeds of doubt, just to name a few.

Whether we acknowledge it or not, our mindset plays a significant role in our success. It shapes how we view setbacks, challenges, failure, and change. But as we've already covered, our mindsets can be drastically affected by society's beliefs and expectations; we can't "fix" these necessarily, but by understanding them we can more effectively manage them and recognize a situation for what it is rather than slipping into the doom spiral of self-judgment.

Let's start with two psychological states, perfectionism and identity foreclosure, that occur internally but are influenced by external factors, particularly in childhood and adolescence, and linger into adulthood, affecting the careers we build.

The Pursuit of Perfection

Perfectionism has been on the rise in the US since the mid 1990s, right alongside the myth of meritocracy. It was no longer enough to attain a four-year degree—that degree now needed to be from a top tier academic institution. As a result, performance on academic testing became paramount to a child's future. And not just performance, but perfection.

Perfectionists thrive in solving straightforward and familiar problems—a behavior that's highly rewarded in childhood education. Kids who are rewarded in academics for their perfectionist behaviors, however, tend to struggle with three things when they enter the professional world:

1. Obsessing over details that don't matter
2. Avoiding unfamiliar situations and difficult tasks that might lead to failure
3. Berating themselves for making mistakes

If perfectionism hinders us, how do we change something so ingrained? Simply telling a perfectionist to focus on doing their best doesn't work. That is too big of an ask, and definitely not straightforward. Instead, research has found that having high personal standards, not pursuing perfectionism, fuels growth. As you continue to accumulate accomplishments, it's natural that your standards will rise.

But simply focusing on our personal standards won't completely eliminate our obsession with perfection, especially since perfectionism is so embedded in our education system. One recommendation is a technique known as mental time travel, in which you look at your current accomplishments from the perspective of your past self. If, five years ago, you could see what you're doing now, how proud of yourself would you be? Mental time travel gives you perspective that can be hard to attain when you're in the thick of burnout or shifting careers.

Identity Foreclosure

Another psychological state fueled by our increasingly competitive career landscape and often shaped during adolescence is identity foreclosure. Identity foreclosure is the commitment to maintain an identity or a set of values prematurely and without compromise.[28] Those with identity foreclosure accept the values that others—like parents, coaches, siblings, or instructors—have placed on them without considering other roles or visions for themselves that they might prefer. Instead of accepting uncertainty about who we want to become, we strengthen the conviction others have handed to us about who we are and what we should want, and then plunge head first into a career path.

As the daughter of Korean immigrants, Eileen Lee explained during our interview that she understood early in life that her duty was to fulfill the American Dream. Growing up, Eileen set her sights on what felt like an obvious path. She would get straight As, be accepted to an Ivy League college, and attend medical school to become a doctor like her father. She was deep in the throes of identity foreclosure until her father passed away suddenly while she was in school.

Eileen found herself completely lost for the first time in her life. Her father had been her rock. She had turned to him for so many answers. In his absence, Eileen realized she didn't know what she really wanted out of life, and perhaps she never had. As painful as it was, losing her father forced Eileen to reexamine her life and assess the differences between what was best for her and what her parents had wanted.

It was another five years of self-examination before Eileen started gaining clarity on where she wanted to make her mark.

The key to reexamining our identities is remembering that they're not set in stone at the start of our lives; they can be reshaped as our beliefs and our lives change. We're not locked in to who we've been if we stay willing to become someone different.

To Be Human is To Be Flawed

This is a bit of a good news/bad news situation. When we open ourselves up to change—be it a shift in our identity or a shift in our career—we face a conundrum: to be human is to have cognitive flaws. These "flaws" aren't personal; they're part of our chemistry. But we need to know what these cognitive flaws and biases are so we can understand how they're affecting our lives—and what we can do about them.

Our brains are incredibly powerful, and when trying to process large amounts of information they default to strategies that help us simplify this information. That's where cognitive biases or flaws come into play. They are unconscious and systematic errors in thinking that influence our decisions and judgments. These biases can distort our perception of reality and fuel inaccurate interpretations of information, keeping us locked in rationally bounded decision-making. By understanding these biases we can recognize them in real-time and take action accordingly. While we won't go through an exhaustive list of these biases, let's look at the ones most likely to keep us stuck.

Status Quo Bias

Have you ever thought about making a change and before you know it you're rattling off all the reasons it won't work? This preference for staying on your current path is called the status quo bias.[29] When facing a decision, we gravitate toward what we know, even if it's undesirable, versus facing the potential risk of the unknown. This ingrained preference for stability makes it difficult to judge alternative options fairly.

Let's use a very common scenario to examine this bias: entertaining the idea of quitting your job. When we look at the prospect of taking action on this idea, we often see all of the unknowns as risks. What if I can't find something better? What if this hurts my career trajectory? What if I go somewhere and it's worse than where I am? What if, what if, what if. We tell ourselves that staying put is starting to look really good. It might not be great—ok, it might be miserable—but at least we know what to expect.

Doing nothing to change our situation doesn't feel like it's as big of a decision or as big of a risk as deciding to act. As humans, we are surprisingly tolerant of pain when we stay the course because of the unknowns associated with making a change. The sneaky part about this bias is that we don't consider inaction to be a decision. We don't consider what we're giving up if we stay the course.

A simple exercise you can do when you catch yourself falling into this pattern is to first acknowledge that, whether you decide to stay or go, you're taking an action either way. Now that you have established this, assess the risk and benefits associated with both actions. Ask yourself, what are the costs/benefits if I leave? What are the costs/benefits if I do nothing? You may still determine that staying is the best decision, but now it is an empowered choice rather than a decision rooted in fear of the unknown.

Escalation of Commitment

As humans, it's our nature to rationalize our decisions, which includes what we have decided as our career path. Think about your career decision like a snowball rolling down a hill. It may have started small, maybe you fell backwards into it or you're just a year in and it wouldn't be hard to make a change or turn back. But, like a snowball growing increasingly larger the further it rolls down the hill, the more you stick to your chosen path, the more days, resources, energy, and effort you invest into this decision.

As you barrel down the hill, your speed picks up and you start seeing all the effort you've already put in to get where you are, even if you're thinking about making a change. You convince yourself to persevere and double down. Momentum is on your side, right? Or is it spiraling faster and faster out of control? At some point, the snowball grows so big that the consequences of making any change feel far too reckless.

That's the escalation of commitment. When faced with the increasing difficulty or potentially negative outcomes of altering our course, we decide to continue our behavior instead.[30] There is no single timeline over which this escalation happens. It might be a two-month interviewing process, a six-month project, or, in Heather Lowey's case, she opened up during an interview that she would spend years at a job she didn't know how to shift out of.

Early in her career, Heather Lowey had her dream

job working for Adidas, where she would be managing the newly announced partnership between the NBA and WNBA. As Adidas evolved their product of apparel for basketball players, Heather was evolving in her career. Over the coming years, Heather would get promoted to Head of Team Services where she continued working with the NBA and WNBA but also NHL, MLS, UFC, and CrossFit.

At some point, though, Heather began to recognize that her identity had gotten tied up in her work. But she loved the job, so was it really that big of a deal? Besides, her coworkers had become more than that to her. They were her friends who had shown up for her when she became a mother three times over and supported her after the tragic loss of her mother. As she reflected on her time at Adidas, she recognized just how entrenched she'd become in her role; "This is what I do and who I am," she told me. The snowball of her career and now her identity was rolling full steam downhill.

After nearly eleven years with the company, Heather began feeling restless. Each time she entertained what this restlessness could mean, she would immediately shut it down. She had a great team, a ton of flexibility, and trust from management and her coworkers that she would always get her job done. She had also reached the highest position in her department. It would be ridiculous to entertain the idea of leaving, right? Heather chided herself for even having these thoughts, prompting more self-doubt. Who was she to complain? She had a job. She got to do cool things at work. Compared to others, she had nothing to complain about.

Heather found herself caught not only in the escalation of commitment, but in the mental trap of comparative suffering too.

Comparative suffering is the act of comparing our own pain or suffering to the pain or suffering of others.[31] Instead of helping, comparative suffering can lead to:

- Denial of our emotions, which can lead to shame, fear, frustration, and loneliness
- Feelings of guilt when we're not suffering as much as others
- Difficulty finding joy in our blessings and accomplishments
- False assumptions about how much better or worse other people have it
- Feeling alone, as though no one understands what we're going through

It turned out that these experiences would become the fuel for Heather's next career move. But that realization was still a few years away.

Binary Bias

Another two years passed, and Heather increasingly felt like she was going through the motions at work. She started volunteering in an effort to silence the whispers of discontent, thinking that might do the trick. But it didn't.

She still felt at a crossroads in her life, and she had no idea how to proceed. To her, all options seemed like bad ones, but she had unknowingly oversimplified those options to black and white, stay or go, same career or radical change. She had fallen into binary bias—our innate instinct to simplify a complex continuum into just two categories in the hopes of gaining clarity or closure.[32]

When we look at a situation like that, of course every choice seems super risky. When we oversimplify, we unintentionally:

1. **Limit our creativity.** By reducing choices down to two extremes, we overlook the potential for innovative solutions that lie in the middle ground.
2. **Neglect our needs.** There are nuances and complexities to every situation, and when we categorize something as either positive or negative, good or bad we miss valuable insight that can inform our best next step or deepen our understanding of ourselves or the situation.
3. **Ignore iterative progress.** Binary bias often leads to an all-or-nothing mindset and the inability to see any movement as progress beside extreme action.

Despite recognizing she was no longer happy in her career, Heather was not willing to make a change. She tried to keep doing things the way she always had, but the more she did this, the less she felt like herself. Then news came that Adidas' partnership with the NBA was ending, and this was the seismic shift Heather needed to get unstuck.

Heather was finally listening to the voice that told her she needed a change, and she started taking action. She spoke with mentors about her current situation, joined a small group of women entering a transitional season in their careers. After much thought and care, Heather resigned from Adidas and committed fully to figuring out her next career move.

Her first step was hiring a coach to help her work through the process of discovering who she was becoming in this next chapter of life. She worked with her coach to create a personal mission statement: “connection through radiating happiness.” She wasn’t sure where that vision would lead her, but for the first time in seventeen years she was willing to not know.

Heather continued the exploration process by taking an assessment to determine what she had loved most about her previous work. While reviewing the findings together, Heather’s coach asked her if she had ever considered a career in coaching. Heather laughed because, until two years ago, she had no idea coaching was even a career. But she was intrigued by the idea; the connections between what she loved to do and what a coach did were undeniable. So Heather set out to explore the field, ultimately deciding to leave her previous career path in the sports apparel industry, get her certification, and become a coach.

If Heather had continued to approach her career with a binary lens, there's no doubt she wouldn't have made a change. Even getting to her decision to pursue coaching as a profession happened one gradual step at a time. Throughout the process, she continued to field interviews, even becoming a candidate for a similar job at another sports apparel company. She knew she was good at what she did, but she also knew she no longer wanted to follow that path. Because she had given herself permission to take the best next step before knowing exactly what her next move would be, Heather was able to create momentum toward coaching as a career and confidently withdraw her candidacy.

There's one more psychological trap that's important for us to discuss when it comes to pivoting in our careers, and this one's a doozy—which is why it gets its very own chapter.

FOUR

A Title Is Your Identity

> "We confuse what we do with who we are—and that confusion costs us dearly."
>
> —Arianna Huffington

"What do you want to be when you grow up?" Most of us likely got this question as a kid from at least one adult or teacher, and it seems innocent enough. But it imprints the message that our careers are an important part of our identity. And they are, but not in the definitive, deterministic way we tend to think of them in adulthood. Michelle Obama beautifully articulates the oddity of this frequently posed question: "I think it's one of the most useless questions an adult can ask a child. As if growing up is finite. As if at some point you become something and that's the end."

Nevertheless, this hyperfocus on our future career path—and, by proxy, our future identity—continued. Fast forward to high school, when guidance counselors started discussing what career you wanted so you could pick out the best school to pursue it. If you went to college, then you likely continued this process with counselors at the university, shaping your course load and finding internships that would help you land that job you wanted all those years ago...when you were a teenager, or maybe even younger.

Ironically, this fixation throughout our education on developing specialized skills for a career does little to affect where we end up. Research has found that even in highly specialized degrees, such as math and science, nearly three quarters of American college graduates go into careers unrelated to their majors.

Still, that fixation on finding and working in our chosen career persists once we join the workforce. What we do, society tells us, defines our identity more than the multiple dimensions of who we are outside of work. Consider the last event you went to where you met new people. Chances are high that one of the first questions you heard sounded very similar to the one you got asked as a kid: "What do you do for work?"

This question, despite its overuse, serves a purpose: labels help us make sense of the world; when we are bombarded with information, labels help us categorize something or someone so we can keep our lives moving and our brains organized. They're not all bad. Sometimes we use labels as a way to find common ground, to make an awkward conversation easier, or to determine where we belong.

The upside of labels is that they allow us to create simplicity in our life. But unchecked, labels can turn from helpful to hurtful, especially when it comes to the labels we use for ourselves.

The Enmeshment Trap

It was January 2018, and Kristin Slink's fintech startup LoanHero had just been acquired. On the surface this was a huge success, as 90% of all startups.[33] She was asked to stay on with the company as the SVP of Product, and her package included additional financial incentives to help the LoanHero team through the transition.

This was a time for celebration and yet Kristin was miserable. After the initial excitement of a successful exit, Kristin realized she was struggling to know her place at the company. "My company was me. I was Kristin, the Founder of LoanHero," she shared with me during our interview. "When I sold my company, it felt like I sold my identity." Kristin was experiencing a common side effect of enmeshment.

Enmeshment or the enmeshment trap is the interweaving of identity with title. Specifically in the work context, psychologists define this trap as the struggle to develop an independent sense of self outside of one's profession. Common signs you might be enmeshed with your career include thinking about work whenever you're not there and bringing up what you do within minutes of meeting someone new.

As access to education has increased, so has the risk of getting caught in the enmeshment trap. More individuals with higher education creates more variation in jobs and therefore more income tiers. Jobs have increasingly become a marker of identity because it's easy to make assumptions about education and income—two variables that can determine one's standing in society and how we're judged. But psychology professor and enmeshment expert, Anne Wilson, cautions us against this tendency: "If you tie [your self-worth] to your career," she writes, "the successes and failures you experience will directly affect your self-worth. And because we live in a society where careers are less likely to be lifelong, if we switch or find ourselves out of a job, it can also become an identity crisis."

This toxic love affair between titles and identities can also lead us to ignore or flat out reject opportunities that fall outside of that identity.

Stay in the Box

Megan had just been promoted to run an entire business unit at her company. The sales organization in this unit had consistently underperformed, and she needed help quickly diagnosing the root issues to get the team back on target. Sales being new to her, she realized she needed help and hired a sales consultant to evaluate the team.

After observing the team and doing some interviews, it became clear to the consultant that the existing sales leader was in over their head. Not just that, but they wouldn't be able to improve fast enough to operate at the level the team needed. This presented a new challenge because, at the time, there was a huge talent shortage and hiring was proving to be a slow process, especially for a critical leadership hire.

As the consultant continued their interviews with the leadership team, they began searching for someone already within the organization who might be a strong sales leader. On one of their calls, they met with Erin, the pre and post sales manager who was currently operating as a player coach. As a coach, Erin managed two teams. The first was the pre-sales solution engineers who provided technical expertise on the product during sales conversations. The second was the post-sales implementation managers who helped new customers set up their platform.

As a player, Erin would join sales discovery calls, run technical demos, and provide key information for RFPs (requests for proposals). Setting up initial meetings and sending out contracts to close the deal were the only things Erin and her team weren't doing. Throughout additional interviews with other team members, Erin was referenced as the "go to" expert on all things related to the customer and the product. Not only was her team critical to the success of the sales team, Erin herself was deeply respected by her team and the trusted advisor to anyone who needed to interact with the customer during the sales process.

Upon learning this, the consultant was thrilled to inform Megan that they had found her sales leader candidate. "No," was Megan's initial response. "I don't think so. Erin doesn't do sales. We need somebody who is strong in sales for this role." The consultant was beside themselves at the strong pushback, despite knowing that hiring practices were still largely based on a candidate's education credentials and previous job titles.

In 2019, the concept of hiring talent based on skills rather than credentials became headline news in corporate America. Executives like IBM's CEO Ginni Rometty were shifting to skill-based hiring and had the data to back up this new strategy. Research showed that skill-based hiring not only resulted in a more diverse talent pool but produced strong performance as well. Unfortunately, there was a lot of buzz around the idea with little action to show for it. A 2023 study of Fortune 500 companies found that nearly 90% failed to ask candidates about their skills so they could align them with current job openings.[34]

But focusing on skills over titles requires more than simply stripping titles and education requirements from a job posting. A systemic change would need to take place, where someone could document their core competencies, performance, and relevant skills. The tragic reality is that, despite data proving a more effective way to hire, companies still default to what's familiar—labels, titles, education. It's unsurprising, then, that employees and candidates evaluate their qualifications through the same lens employers use.

Still, the consultant was confident in their recommendation, so they took a new approach. The consultant presented documentation of Erin's skills that aligned with the core job responsibilities of a sales leader to the executive. The consultant watched the information sink in, and a smile crossed Megan's face; she had found her sales leader.

But Megan wasn't the only one putting Erin in a box. When they approached Erin about the sales leader position, her first reaction was to say, "I'm not in sales." Again, the consultant was taken aback by her response. She identified so much with her role as pre and post sales that she never considered how her rich expertise aligned perfectly with this new role. Once again, making a change wasn't just a career move but an identity shift. Despite already doing a large portion of the role, Erin perceived her seemingly minor experience gaps as big risks.

Nevertheless, Erin decided to take the role, and within weeks any concern about making the change was replaced with confidence as the team began to thrive under her guidance.

There's one more way that titles can affect how we see ourselves and our skill sets—especially when it comes to evaluating our perceived abilities.

Domain Dependence

In 2020, I was invited to run a sales workshop for female tech founders. Each of them was at a point in their company where they had defined the market, defined the problem, built at least a minimally viable product, and now needed to drive revenue through customer acquisition. None of these founders held a sales title in their previous jobs. When I polled the room on their impression of sales, the resounding theme was that sales just wasn't something they would be good at or that sales conflicted with who they were as a person. I had my work cut out for me.

Even though I knew the answer, I asked how many of the founders sold prior to launching their startup. No hands went up. Then I asked them a series of questions; had they done any of these specific behaviors? (Spoiler alert, these are all sales skills):

- Have you asked questions to understand a situation better?
- Have you taught someone something new?
- Have you convinced someone to support your idea?

With each question, all hands in the room went up. Each of these founders had used sales skills previously but they didn't recognize them as such, nor had they transferred their previous experience with these skills into their current endeavor of acquiring customers.

I asked one of the founders to elaborate on a time when she had asked questions to better understand a situation. She proceeded to tell me about her process for customer discovery, in which she tested her hypothesis about what her target customer cared about. During customer discovery, she asked a series of questions to confirm the pain point her company sought to address. Next, she would share ideas for how the customer could solve the challenges they were facing, then she would ask them for feedback on those ideas. By the end of the call, she typically had a sense for their willingness (or unwillingness) to pay for a solution to their challenge. Without realizing it, she had already used several sales skills throughout her customer discovery process—a connection she was able to see by the end of the workshop.

This phenomenon—failing to recognize the similarity between skills and situations outside of the context in which we learned them—is called domain dependence.[35] Once they learned about this, the founders at my workshop were able to claim their past experiences as skills that had been there all along. Each one walked out with a newfound confidence that she could, indeed, do sales for her company because she had already successfully done so in the past—just not under the "sales" domain.

By understanding the various psychological flaws and phenomena we've covered in these last two chapters, you'll be able to recognize them when they crop up. And crop up they will—especially when considering a big change in your life.

Before examining the ways the workplace isn't made for women, I want you to remember this moving forward:

Your future is not determined by your current domain. You are not your job title. You don't have to stay true to your childhood answer of what you wanted to be when you grew up. You have more than two binary options, and you don't have to be the most miserable person at work before you consider changing your role or career. The status quo, the identity you've had for years—these things don't have to determine your next steps. You get to do that. And you get to do that knowing all these cognitive flaws and societal scripts will come into play as you consider what you want to pursue in your next chapter. That's not a bad thing; it's just a human thing. And now you're prepared to face them when they join you on your journey.

FIVE

The Workplace Is Not Built For Or By You

"If you can't see the system, you'll always think the problem is you."

—Ann Helen Petersen

The twentieth century brought radical changes to the composition of the professional workplace. Despite key legislature and technological advancements that helped pave the path for more women to join and stay in the workforce, social conditioning and gender biases were far more difficult to dismantle.

If you're having a particularly difficult time examining your career or knowing where you want to head next, you're not alone. As a woman you face different issues, and we're about to discuss why.

We've Come So Far?

At the start of the 1900s, it was uncommon for women to work, especially once they married. In fact, just 20% of all US women and 5% of married women worked outside the home.[36] Technological advancements in the 1950s brought in the first round of advancement for women in the workplace, creating a new category of work known as clerical professions. Clerical roles, such as secretary, receptionist, and admin assistant, were often temporary and did not require a four-year degree; perfect roles for women, the men in charge decided. Temp agencies like Manpower (yes, Manpower) emerged to staff these new positions, specifically seeking out white women to fill them.

While it was still not widely acceptable for white women to work outside the home, agencies like Manpower made sure to protect any male egos possibly offended by the idea of working alongside women by emphasizing the temporary, optional nature of their roles. Women simply wanted extra spending money, they argued, and could return to full-time housewife at any point. Despite this narrative, the door was now open, and women's participation in the workplace more than doubled over the next thirty years.[37]

In the 1970s, Ivy Leagues such as Brown, Princeton, and Yale, who had long been male-only institutions, began admitting female students. Contrary to what Manpower believed, many women didn't return to full-time housewife, even after having kids. These two factors brought about a resurgence of women pursuing higher education—a trend that continues today, with 58% of undergrad degrees and 62% of master's degrees earned by women.[38]

As the face of corporate America changed, so did legislation. New regulations were introduced, including the Pregnancy Discrimination Act in 1978, as a way to prohibit discrimination on the basis of pregnancy, childbirth, or related medical conditions. A less obvious but equally impactful legislation was the establishment of Title IX in 1972. Title IX provided everyone with equal access to any program or activity that received federal funding, most notably improving opportunity for women in sports. Research found that experience in sports both increased women's self-esteem and their future participation in male-dominated, higher pay occupations.

For the first time in history, women were expanding beyond traditionally female fields, such as teaching, nursing, and clerical work, and entering male-dominated careers as doctors, lawyers, engineers, and managers. While there were several early wins, the rate of progress quickly plateaued in the decades that followed, despite a continuous pipeline of ambitious, career-driven women joining the workplace. Although women now make up 47% of the workforce,[39] we're alarmingly absent in leadership positions—a lack that has nothing to do with either performance or qualification, research shows. Over the last five years, there has been single digit growth of women in leadership at every level of the leadership pipeline. Women only represent 10.6% of Fortune 500 CEOs,[40] and they only hold just 28% of executive leadership positions.[41]

Why this discrepancy despite firms with more women in senior positions being more profitable, more socially responsible, and better providers of safer, higher quality customer experiences? The answer is all too simple and all too familiar: equal access does not mean equal treatment.

According to Pew Research Center, 56% of men believe sexism in the US has been eliminated; 63% of women say it still affects them on a regular basis.[42] The kicker? The more that individuals believe they're not biased, the more likely they are to exhibit biased behavior.

Women are still operating in a system that was neither built for them or by them. There are centuries of deeply entrenched biases and gender expectations that have been imprinted on us, often without our permission. We're going to examine these biases and expectations in more detail so that, as you strategize your next career move, you have a better understanding of the "rules" at play. They were not made with you in mind or, if they were, they were made to keep you out of the game.

This is not meant to deflate you but to help you recognize situations for what they are. While this chapter is not an exhaustive list of the biases women face in the workplace, it does highlight the most likely challenges you'll encounter.

Glass Cliffs and Ceilings

At the first company I worked for, we had two powerhouse female VPs who we'll call Kim and Jessica. Kim was the VP of Corporate and Consumer Marketing, and when I joined the company she had already been there for nine years. When she joined as the business development manager, the company was a small tech startup; now she was touted as someone critical to the company's success, and it was easy to see why.

She had quickly proved her aptitude as a strong performer and exceptional relationship builder when she sold and managed key strategic partnerships that established the startup as a dominant player in the industry. Next, she headed up the acquisition of three companies and established an east coast office in NYC. From there, she was promoted to VP of Client Service and Strategy where she oversaw the entire go to market teams for the online media, promotions, and data businesses before becoming VP of Marketing and Media. In this new role, she drove revenue growth by 28% on a $40 million book of business and handled all corporate communication surrounding the IPO of the company.

She knew the business in and out, and people across the organization saw her as the go-to voice of the company. Despite being looked to by the executive team for guidance on strategic decisions, she continued having male executives parachuted in over her. These actions spoke much louder than the praise she received for her work. She had hit the glass ceiling at a company that was still very much a boy's club at the executive and board level.

The glass ceiling is a metaphor representing the invisible barrier that prevents women and people of color from advancing upward in the workplace despite their qualifications.[43] The glass ceiling starts at the first rung of management, where the most recent numbers show that for every one hundred men promoted, only eighty-seven women are promoted, and just eighty-two women of color are promoted.[44] In the eight years that McKinsey & Company have tracked these numbers, there has been little to no improvement at any level of leadership despite more women entering the workforce and outpacing men in college graduation rates and higher education degrees.

Joan C. Williams coined this phenomenon the Prove-It-Again Bias. Women get asked, again and again, to prove their competency while men are evaluated on their potential. In an analysis of recommendation letters for medical faculty, women's accomplishments were repeatedly attributed to hard work while men's accomplishments were attributed to brilliance. The recommendation letters for women used terms like "caring" or "compassionate" and referenced their personal lives four times more than the recommendation letters for men.

In the tech industry, the Center for Talent Innovation found that 40% of women were leaving tech companies after a decade in the industry compared to just 17% of men. Their primary reasons for leaving the industry had nothing to do with family demands or satisfaction with the job. Rather, the report cited reasons like "undermining behavior from managers" and "a sense of feeling stalled in one's career." Clear indications of hitting that glass ceiling.

There's another phenomenon called the glass cliff, in which women are appointed or promoted to higher positions during a time of crisis. Researchers found that women were 63% more likely to be recruited into leadership roles than men when those positions were already unstable.[45] While these positions create opportunities for women to prove themselves yet again, there is also a heightened risk of career damaging consequences should they take these opportunities. Beyond increased levels of stress and burnout, women who are unable to turn things around fast enough during these crises are judged more harshly, seen as less competent, and face more severe penalties, including losing status.

Consider the rise and fall of Chief Diversity Officers in recent years. In the wake of George Floyd's murder, there was a huge push for companies to make diversity a priority. Chief Diversity Officer positions were added to the C-Suite seemingly overnight so companies could at least pay lip service to making a change. But truly prioritizing diversity in the workplace was (and still is) a huge undertaking that required organizational change at every level, alignment across entire companies, uprooting outdated beliefs, education on entrenched biases, and strategies to replace those biases.

Women make up 54.5% of Chief Diversity Officer positions,[46] a number which has increased twenty percent in the last decade with the rapid rise of the role. Not surprisingly, these leaders have been more vulnerable to layoffs than their human resources counterparts because they were brought in during a time of crisis, experiencing 40% higher turnover.[47] Placing women in positions of leadership during already tumultuous times only further exacerbates the outdated belief that stereotypically male traits lend themselves best to leadership.

The Maternal Wall

The maternal wall is the assumption that mothers are either uncommitted to their jobs if they take time off to care for their families or cold and uncaring if they don't.[48] Sadly, the maternal wall bias is not isolated to a single industry—it affects women's chances of being hired regardless of the field they're in. A study conducted at Stanford by sociologist Shelley Correll sought to determine if simply being a mother would impact a hiring decision. Participants in the study were given two nearly identical resumes to evaluate. There was just one minor difference: one applicant was a mother and the other was not. Nonmothers received 2.1 times more callbacks and were recommended for hire 1.8 times more than mothers.

A 2014 New York Times article further exacerbated the issue by cautioning readers that "one of the worst career moves a woman can make is to have children."[49]

Women not only face the maternal wall, they also face the motherhood penalty, where a woman's pay decreases if she becomes a mother. On average, mothers make 63 cents for every dollar paid to fathers. Even full-time employed mothers make 71 cents for every dollar made by a father. Compared to women without children, mothers are given job offers where the compensation, on average, is $11,000 less.

Researchers have found that parenthood may alter earning potential between genders as well, as parenthood tends to reinforce traditional gender roles. The belief is that men feel a greater responsibility to provide for their family, therefore increasing their commitment to work, whereas women feel compelled to spend more time on domestic tasks, making them less committed to work. Men, by contrast, do not suffer a penalty when they become dads. In fact, there's some evidence of a "fatherhood bonus," in which their earnings actually increase.

Unfortunately, simply not having children doesn't protect women from the maternal wall bias. A survey of five hundred managers found that even women who were deemed to be in the "fertility zone" faced discrimination. 40% of managers admitted to being reluctant to hire a woman in the "fertility zone," and nearly one third said they would prefer to hire men in their twenties and thirties to avoid the potential costs of maternity leave.[50]

Be More Like A Man

The second VP, Jessica, had a similar trajectory as Kim, but her experience was on the B2B (business to business) side of the company. Jessica started as a customer support rep, and in her first four years with the company she was promoted four times, eventually becoming Director of Customer Services. It looked like her star was rising fast within the company, and she continued to excel in each of the roles she took on.

Curious to learn more about the customer acquisition side of the business, Jessica moved out of customer support leadership and became a sales manager. Again, she saw tremendous growth, earning two promotions over the next three years and eventually becoming VP of Sales, where she was responsible for over $100M in revenue and a sales organization of over 125 reps.

Part of why Jessica was so beloved by her team was her reputation as a people-first leader, and openings within her organization were highly coveted. However, the further Jessica rose up the org chart, the more she was encouraged to change her personality. This pressure was particularly evident when it came time to do the Insights Discovery personality assessment, which was part of the company's leadership development program. This assessment was intended to help leaders become more self-aware of their unique style and abilities.

After answering a series of intensive questions, the assessment places participants on a color wheel. There are four primary personality colors: red, yellow, blue, and green. The assessment was a big deal at this company, with the senior leaders' colors widely known and shared. Nearly all of the executives were some shade of red. Although the assessment used a color wheel, the company saw green and red as opposites. Greens were known for their caring, encouraging, patient, sharing, and relaxed traits while reds were known for their competitive, demanding, determined, strong-willed, and purposeful traits. Hard not to see how these colors bore a strong resemblance to stereotypical gender traits.

Jessica originally tested green when she landed in her new VP role and was actively coached into being more "red" like the other senior leaders. This campaign to turn Jessica's greenish hues to red was both widely known and talked about in the leadership team—and no one batted an eye at the obvious gender dynamics at play. It was clear to them that if someone wanted to be an executive at the company, they needed to test red. After several years, Jessica "finally" made herself into a red (or gamed the test) in the hopes that she would earn a spot on the executive team. Spoiler alert, she never rose higher than VP; meanwhile, the active coaching intended to diminish the traits that made her such a remarkable leader continued.

Besides the obvious ick factor of telling women to exhibit more masculine traits to advance their careers, this advice has proven to be incredibly harmful to women. Society sees the behaviors often associated with leadership, such as assertiveness, confidence, and authority, as norm violations when exhibited by a woman. Women are expected to be kind, friendly, humble, and socially skilled.

This puts women in a double bind, where it's impossible to be viewed as a leader if they lack the stereotypical traits of one, and yet, if they're assertive and confident, they're penalized for being "too masculine." A review of student ratings for professors in higher education found that female professors received lower ratings for not being sufficiently warm and accessible; however, when they were warm and accessible, they were penalized for not being authoritative or professional.[51]

Another type of "norm violation" occurs when women excel in traditionally male fields. This is seen as an anomaly—and not one in which women are viewed favorably. There is a famous study known as the Heidi/Howard Case Study. Columbia Business School Professor Frank Flynn wanted to test the impact of gender in the workplace, so he built a case study based on a real Silicon Valley venture capital investment partner named Heidi Roizen. For reference, women still made up just 11% of investment partners in 2018. Safe to consider this a male-dominated field.

Flynn presented half the class with Heidi's information; to the other half of the class, he presented Heidi's information too, except he changed the name from Heidi to Howard. Then he asked the class how these "two" people compared to each other. Heidi and Howard were rated equally in competence, but Heidi was thought to be too aggressive and selfish; few students wanted to work for or hire her as a result. Howard, on the other hand, was viewed as someone who would make a great colleague, even a great boss. This study shone a spotlight directly at the consequences women face when they're seen as violating society's gender norms.

Biased Assessments and Feedback

A 2014 study analyzed 248 performance reviews from 180 managers in the tech industry to assess how they judged employee behavior. On average, managers were critical of employee performance in 58.9% of men's reviews and 87.9% of the women's reviews.[52] Women were repeatedly scrutinized for their personality and communication skills, and the word "abrasive" was used in seventy-one of the ninety-four critical reviews of women evaluated in the study.

Here are just some of the ways women's strengths are given back to them.

STRENGTH	WHAT YOU'RE TOLD
You allow others to be in the spotlight	You lack confidence
You seek a solution that works for both parties involved	You are indecisive
You will sacrifice personal accolades for the greater good	You are not competitive
You provide context to data to provide an accurate picture	You ramble and are not succinct
You care about people and how things impact them	You are too sensitive or emotional

Like Jessica experienced, these gender norms are baked into the code of personality assessments, which are then used to determine leadership potential. Or, more likely than not, keep women out of leadership.

I was working with a coaching client who had recently taken the Hogan assessment while working as an emerging executive for a Fortune 500 company. The Hogan assessment is similar to Insights Discovery or Myers Briggs and claims to provide "the depth and detail needed to hire the right employees, identify and develop talented individuals, and build better leaders."

When she first read her results from the assessment, she was surprised at her lower than average ranking on ambition. It felt misaligned with who she knew herself to be. She had always had a strong drive to achieve professional success, and she had a big vision of the global impact she would have throughout her career. Something was not adding up, so she asked the specialist who deployed the assessments for more insight on how ambition was scored.

She learned that Hogan's ambition score measured the degree to which a person seems socially self-confident, leaderlike, competitive, and energetic, or, conversely, the degree to which a person is laid back, flexible, noncompetitive, and a good team player. The assessment, it seems, is riddled with bias that favors stereotypical male traits, and yet it continues to be used by 75% of Fortune 500 companies to inform their hiring, development, and identification of future leaders. It's not hard to imagine the damaging ripple effects this assessment has had on the countless women who've taken it, only to receive faulty feedback that they're not ambitious enough to be considered a future executive.

The likelihood that your career trajectory has been or will be impacted simply because of your gender is highly likely. This isn't a reflection of who you are; it's a reflection of society's expectations of women. As women, it's important to understand the all too real headwinds we still face in the workplace—not so we feel defeated and demoralized (although it's perfectly fine to be furious) but so we know what we're up against.

When we know the biases working against us, we can then develop a strategy for how to move forward. Knowledge allows us to make empowered choices.

2

CAREER CHANGE IS A RIGHT OF PASSAGE

Linear Careers ≠ Normal

If you've ever felt that changing your career would make you an anomaly among other professionals, you are not alone in that illusion. Even those who have made just one career change will tell you that their career path is unusual.

Researchers from Harvard Graduate School of Education were intrigued by individuals who had achieved impressive success and found fulfillment in their careers by taking a distinctly circuitous path. At the start of their research, they worried it would be difficult to find enough of these seemingly rare professionals for their study. They cast a wide net, assuming that only 20% of applicants would meet the criteria. Instead, they were flooded with qualified participants. Forty-five of the first fifty applicants described winding career paths. Already they had a surprising finding: nonlinear careers for successful professionals were far more prevalent than expected. This study became known as the Dark Horse Project.

It's All an Illusion

In psychology, there's something called the "end of history illusion." It's that quirky ability humans have to look at our past and realize how much we've changed; but when we consider the future, we assume we'll change very little, if at all. When we look at careers through the lens of human psychology, it seems obvious, even logical, that our careers naturally evolve over time. As adults, though, regardless of our age or stage of life, psychologists Gilbert, Quoidbach, and Wilson found that "people regard the present as a watershed moment at which they have finally become the person they will be for the rest of their lives."[53]

That's all well and good, except that decades of research on personality development have proven that the only constant in our lives is change. Psychologist Dr. Brent Roberts aggregated ninety-two studies on personality development to find patterns of continuity and change in personality traits across adulthood. He discovered there were some traits that evolved predictably, including a correlation between aging and becoming more agreeable, conscientious, emotionally stable, and less neurotic. While we experience the most momentous changes between between eighteen and late twenties, we never stop changing. It's not surprising, then, that a career you chose in your early twenties is no longer aligned with who you're becoming now.

As a driven professional, it's tempting to believe you alone write your career path and shape your future. As a high achiever, chances are you've usually been able to set a goal and achieve it. You may have been a former subscriber to the myth of meritocracy; you may still want to believe that if you work hard and do a great job you will be a success. Unknowingly, you have fallen for the illusion that you are in control of your career. For many, however, a day comes when things change that are not on your terms and a decision is made for you that alters your career forever. You are no longer the sole author of your professional path, and this can feel incredibly destabilizing.

A 10-year study of over 2,600 executives found that 45% would be fired at least once. The study also discovered that 91% of the executives who faced a major setback found something just as good if not better than what they had been doing prior to the setback.[54]

A forced change to a career doesn't always come in the form of termination. It could be that your incredible company goes through a major acquisition. You begin noticing changes in policies and leadership, and maybe your role is impacted too. Other times, it may be that your boss gets replaced and you need to figure out a new operating rhythm, or perhaps you're part of a massive layoff. Change to your career could even come in the form of a global pandemic, as so many of us experienced in 2020. While the change, whatever prompts it, may not be of your choosing, it can still serve you and your career.

For over a decade, Kate Van Waes meticulously crafted a career in academia. She earned a Master's and PhD at Brown University, completed her first post doc in Switzerland and her second post doc working on the NASA Mars Reconnaissance Orbiter team. Although she didn't enjoy the heavy research focus of her projected path, she hoped she would just learn to deal with it. She had already invested so much into this career; was it really a big deal if she didn't love it? At the time, Kate didn't realize she was falling into the all too common bias of escalating commitment, despite getting early signals that this career might not be for her. But she continued down the path until one day she found herself in a position she never expected.

With her eyes set on tenure track, she began applying for professor positions at various universities. This happened to be in 2008, and the global economic crisis brought her world to a screeching halt. Overnight, all of the universities put freezes on tenured professor positions with no line in sight when they would return. Kate found herself without job prospects, a way to pay rent, and the very real possibility that she might've just spent a decade on a career that was no longer viable.

As she shared her predicament with friends, she learned about the American Association for Advancement of Science Fellowship Program which took PhD scientists like

Kate and placed them in the government. Hopeful that this could be a perfect layover until the economy bounced back and she could try again for a tenure track professor position, Kate went through the rigorous application and interview process. Unbeknownst to her, that decision would forever change the trajectory of her career.

Kate was accepted into the program and quickly discovered a whole new world in government where she flourished. In this new environment, Kate discovered skills she had not flexed in her previous career. She learned she was adept at seeing the big picture, distilling it down, and quickly making a decision. She also discovered just how many decisions were made by talking things out in meetings and coming to a collective decision. Her new environment was the complete opposite of academia, so she didn't expect her lightbulb moment of realizing that this was what she was meant to do.

A forced change set Kate on a career path she might not have chosen for herself, but that change gave her the chance to explore. During the Great Recession, she found a work environment where her strengths and skills aligned perfectly with her new role. Because of the unexpected, Kate was free to create incredible job satisfaction and success down a path she never intended to pursue.

This would not be the last career change for Kate, but now she knew that change, while it might not be of her choosing, could still serve her.

A Shared Experience

As the Dark Horse Project got underway, researchers again stumbled upon a surprising discovery. Despite their vastly different backgrounds, each of the applicants shared the belief that they were an anomaly and expressed embarrassment about jumping around so much in their careers.

The fact that even highly successful and respected professionals still felt ashamed about their unconventional paths is a direct reflection of the chasm in our working culture between reality and perceived reality. The perceived reality is that successful people choose one career and stick with it, no matter what. The reality is that many successful people follow nonlinear paths. This creates a vicious catch-22, in which professionals don't want to expose their unconventional careers because they believe they're highly unusual. Because they don't share about their experiences, other professionals who are also following nonlinear paths believe they're alone; there are no nonlinear role models that they can see, leading them to believe the true path to success is a linear one and theirs is an anomaly. It's a brutal cycle of career shame and silence.

The Dark Horse Project did not just debunk this myth, it illuminated the underlying patterns in these seemingly unique, disconnected career paths. Researchers learned that what had fueled success for the professionals in their study was a willingness to make changes and prioritize fulfillment. "Here's who I am at the moment, here are my motivations, here's what I've found I like to do, here's what

I'd like to learn, and here are the opportunities. Which of these is the best match right now?"

The Dark Horse Project highlighted how common it is for our career paths to be varied and nonlinear, and it answered what had fueled the success of these individuals—a willingness to change and prioritize their fulfillment—but the study left out a key aspect of making a career change: How had they actually done it? Even if you were ready for a change, there is rarely a map detailing what steps to take.

A common misconception when we're at this juncture is to look outside ourselves for answers. We may try consulting with mentors, family, or friends, hoping they have insight into our next best move. We attend webinars and events featuring speakers who share how they made a change. These sources can certainly be helpful, but the truth is that no one has your answer but you. In fact, becoming overly reliant on what others think is one of the fastest ways to find yourself misaligned and headed in the wrong direction. If no two paths are the same, your trusted network does not have your answer, and if it's unclear what steps you should take next, then how are you supposed to get unstuck?

By following a process.

By remembering that changing careers is a right of passage—a signal of growth, not an anomaly or a shameful decision.

Changing careers is a signal that you're choosing to

embrace who you are becoming rather than fighting to stay who you were.

We grow and change throughout the course of our lives. Our priorities shift. And our career aspirations and interests will change as we grow. Unfortunately, our working culture doesn't yet understand or celebrate this as a beautiful signal of growth, not a deviation, a one-off, a fluke.

But you're not the first person to navigate this process, and those who have gone before you have paved the way. Let's turn the page and embark on a guided journey of finding ourselves, where the answers lie within but you don't have to travel alone anymore either.

SIX

Roadmap to Unstuck

"The path isn't linear. It's a spiral, bringing us back to the same place but with deeper understanding."

—Elizabeth Lesser

Denise Odenkirk was an accomplished supply chain executive with over twenty years' experience in the healthcare industry. She was well respected in her field, but her current line of work no longer held her interest the way it had before, despite reaching tremendous success. She sensed a desire for change, but she put all of her focus on work and family rather than inspect the feeling closer. Then, a few months later at a work conference hosted by GHX, a software vendor she had used for years, she was struck by a very clear thought: "This is a company I want to be a part of."

At first she was surprised by the voice. There was no doubt she was a huge fan of the company. She had advocated to implement their software at multiple organizations. As a long-time customer, Denise had built strong relationships with the leadership team at GHX and felt a strong connection to them and the culture they had established at the company. She considered the CEO to be a friend—someone she could reach out to directly. But this was the first time she felt a strong pull to not just work with this company but to work for them. Was this perhaps the answer to the voice saying she was ready for something more? By the end of the conference, Denise knew this was her next step, but she had no idea how or when it would happen.

When she returned from the conference, Denise couldn't wait to share her epiphany with her husband. He had been a huge supporter of her career, and he knew she'd been feeling restless. Her husband listened attentively as Denise enthusiastically explained how this move made sense as a next step in her career. When she finished, he encouraged her to pursue the path if it was something she truly wanted. Then he brought up a detail Denise had overlooked in her excitement. Their kids were at an age where they had made close friends, they were heavily involved in activities, and Denise and her husband agreed that her next role would be in Virginia where they lived. This company was based out of Colorado.

Rather than be deterred by this realization, they asked themselves what would it look like if Denise could work for this company and keep the family's home base in Virginia. As they explored their options, they decided that his job gave them enough flexibility for Denise to travel regularly if she needed to. With the first hurdle cleared, Denise set her sights on figuring out what she could do at the company that would allow her to work remotely and align with her skills.

An answer began to emerge as she reflected on what brought her joy and excitement. She knew she was deeply passionate about GHX's solution; she had been crucial in selling it internally at the companies where she worked. Her deep expertise in healthcare supply chains meant she uniquely understood GHX's customer voice. She was also passionate about leadership and had built high performing teams at all of her past companies. As she looked at her skills and expertise, coupled with her need to work remotely, the area to focus her efforts became clear. What about sales? While she had never formally worked as a sales professional, she recognized that her skill set and experience transferred well in the industry.

The picture was becoming clearer. Now it was time to test if this idea could become a reality. Denise reached out to the CEO of GHX. Given their prior relationship, he happily found time to meet with Denise, who shared that she wanted GHX to be the next chapter in her career, although she wasn't sure exactly how or what she would do. She explained that she needed to work out of Virginia but could travel if necessary.

The CEO listened intently; he was open to exploring options. "Do you have something specific in mind?" he asked once she finished explaining. "Sales," Denise replied without hesitation.

Although he was surprised an operations leader would entertain a career change to sales, they ended that first call with the intention to continue exploring roles that would fit Denise's needs and skills. Over the coming months, Denise and the CEO continued brainstorming, eventually landing on an individual contributor sales role working with their top customers—a role that would both meet her criteria and fill a need for GHX.

Despite all the planning, this career move felt a little risky. It would mean taking a step out of leadership after nearly twenty years. But Denise knew she had done the work to understand what she wanted, which was to be part of GHX. She also knew that when she was passionate about her work she could drive incredible outcomes, and she trusted that her time with GHX would be no different.

In May of 2013, Denise made arguably the biggest change in her career and accepted the job at GHX. Turns out, her belief that she would find her way back to leadership was well founded. Within a year in her role, Denise was promoted into senior leadership as the VP of Supplier Sales where she has continued to thrive.

The Process

Denise's journey is just one example of the process of

making a career change. Let's break down the five stages of getting unstuck using Denise's story.

1. **A Seed is Planted.** You may have known it for a while, but this is the moment when you accept that you need a change. The change itself is still unclear, but you're now committed to giving life to this voice. For Denise, this moment happened when she attended the GHX conference and realized it was where she was meant to go next. She was good at her current job, but she had lost her passion for it and was ready for a new challenge. That conference planted the seed.
2. **Exploration.** During exploration, you turn to your internal foundation for insight into what the change might be. Your internal foundation is an understanding of your strengths, priority life dimension, energy givers/takers, and key themes from your life and career. If you do not have an internal foundation yet, stay open. Gather new information—about yourself, your needs and responsibilities, and where you thrive best. Denise understood that both her career and her relationships were critical dimensions of her life at the time. Through her experience working with GHX, she knew their culture aligned with her personal core values. She also took time to reflect on the type of work that gave her energy and where she had developed deep expertise and skills. This

information would be essential as she progressed to the next stage.

3. **Activation.** Until this point in the process, you've been on a largely internal journey. This is the first stage where you begin involving your trusted network and communicating what you uncovered during exploration. There were two key interactions Denise highlighted as part of this stage. The first was sharing her ideas with her husband and collaborating on what worked best for their family. The second was meeting with the CEO of GHX where she articulated her interest in joining the company, addressed potential "blockers," like in her need to stay in Virginia, and brainstormed ideas for what type of role might be a fit. These conversations laid the groundwork for the next stage.
4. **Build and Test.** Here you get to experiment and explore your options. Just because you try something doesn't mean it will be the change you're seeking, but all of your tests will help you gather valuable information for getting unstuck. While Denise continued working full time, she and the CEO at GHX began testing different job possibilities. Through this process, they were able to get a sense of what was appealing to Denise and helpful at the company, and what was a hard no for both parties. They went through several ideas before landing on the best fit.

5. **Commit.** Although you have been working toward this moment, committing can still be the most difficult stage to complete. The final step of making a career change is crossing the bridge of calculated risk (more on this later) and fully committing to the change. As Denise approached this stage, she knew she had done everything in her control to make the right decision. Even with all the insights she gathered, there were still unknowns about how the new role would actually go. Would she be able to sell? What if she was unable to get back to an executive level after taking this step back? There was plenty of room for her inner critic to grab the microphone, but because Denise had built a strong foundation and gone through these stages, she was able to recall the facts of everything she had learned about herself, her values, and her priorities; she knew this was the best next step. So she trusted herself and committed to the change.

Many of you are likely reading this book because you're either stuck or you're entering that first stage: a seed has been planted, and you're not sure what to do next. Knowing the stages of making a meaningful career change is important, but equally important is understanding that sneaky thoughts, emotions, and even resistance can creep in as you embark on this journey.

Since you're not alone on the path anymore, let's turn to the helpful reminders left for us to glean from the women who have come before and made a similar decision to change. Here's what they—and I—want you to know:

You Already Know How To Do This

Picture a current project or challenge you're tackling at work. I'm guessing that if I asked you what your next one or two steps are, you would quickly rattle them off. Even if the final solution isn't clear yet, you know that things will begin to take shape by gathering information. You enlist help from people who have information you might need, and you gather any data that can help ground your decisions in facts. At some point, you likely have to make a decision without all of the information.

While you may view exploring any type of shift in your current career as risky, the reality is that you are already well equipped to navigate this process. You've already done it, just under different circumstances.

There Is Always a Move To Make

The beauty of a career is that there's rarely a choice or decision you can't come back from. Outside of death, nothing is permanent. Which means your career is flexible and fluid. It can adapt as you grow, your priorities shift, or you recognize misalignment. You are not stuck. There is always a move you can make.

It's important to call out that finding your place of alignment may take multiple iterations. You may need to take a series of best next steps in order to find a good fit in your career. The key is trusting that if you continue to show up and do the work you will get there.

Sometimes Things Fall Apart So They Can Fall Into Place

This transition of navigating between a past that is clearly over and a future that is uncertain is known as a liminal state. The very root of the word "transition" is "transit," which means to take a voyage from one place to another. Being in transit means accepting that we are in the process of leaving one thing, without having fully left it, while simultaneously beginning something without fully being a part of it yet.

It takes time to understand what you want to change, recognize the beliefs or assumptions keeping you stuck, and develop skill sets and relationships in a new arena. In her book *Working Identity*, Herminia Ibarra attributes the difficulty of this transitional state to "juggling lots of different things—not necessarily with great coherence or consistency." As we dive deeper into exploring ourselves and our opportunities, it's expected that we'll "begin to feel fragmented, not whole."

As you go through this transition, know that feeling fuzzy, unclear, and even disoriented is all part of the process. Messiness is simply a signal that you're doing a great job and getting where you are meant to be.

Facts Over Feelings

It is surprisingly scary to let go of our outdated beliefs, even when we know they don't serve us. These fears are distinctly different from that deep sense of knowing yourself and where you work and operate best. These outdated beliefs often come out in statements that sound like, "Oh I couldn't do that" or "I'm not good at x" or "But that one thing has always fueled my ambition."

These beliefs may be things we've determined about ourselves for a variety of reasons, some even stemming from one-off comments we heard as a child or young adult. We carry these beliefs with us, even seeking out information to affirm them rather than actively challenging them.

As your beliefs surface in this process, ask yourself, "Do you think or do you know?" Sit with the answer. Be as honest as possible with yourself. Do you actually know that thing to be true based on facts and experiences, or is it an assumption you're making or someone else's leftover opinion? If your answer includes any assumptions, the next question is, "What steps can I take to find the answer?" This strategy is a great way to rein in that inner critic trying to keep you small or undermine your potential. Rather than giving it life, you can now approach that voice with curiosity and challenge its message.

You can update your outdated narratives and beliefs. You are not who you were, or who they said you were. You are someone who lets herself change and grow.

SEVEN

Outside The Box

"You can't really know where you are going until you know where you have been."

—Maya Angelou

Imagine meeting a new professional connection for coffee. Once you exhaust small talk about the weather, you inevitably get some version of "So tell me about you." When this happens, your brain likely kicks into overdrive: "What should I say? How much do I include? How do I capture everything without talking for the next twenty minutes?" One of a few scenarios happens next.

You might start detailing the various aspects of your career, and after talking for what feels like a long time, you can sense the other person, although smiling and nodding, is struggling to follow along. In an attempt to get things back on track you hear yourself saying, "Sorry for rambling so much." or worse, "I know. It is a bit random." Then you quickly try to shift the conversation away from you.

Or maybe you have a go-to elevator pitch that grossly oversimplifies your experience but hits on all the things that people can grab onto, like where you grew up, where you went to college, big brands you worked for, and your current title. When you're done, you quickly issue a follow-up to the person you're speaking with.

Or maybe you become a mirror. You ask the other person to go first so that you can get a sense of how they answer the question. How long do they take? Did they share anything about their personal life? When it's your turn, you adapt your introduction to mimic what they just shared.

Each of these scenarios highlights the same challenge: we are more concerned about what others think of us than being our true selves and owning our stories. According to social psychologist Amy Cuddy, this behavior is exactly what keeps us from showing up with presence. She defines presence as "the state in which we stop worrying about the impression we're making on others and start being our best selves." Her research found that it's not enough to know or even affirm our story—we must trust it. When we trust our story, we shed the pressure to "fit in", and we own the narrative.

People will believe you because you believe in your story. But in order to own our story, we first have to connect the dots. You know the pivotal moments that shaped your life and career, but others won't until you understand how it fits together and draw the connecting lines for them.

Connecting the Dots

Humans are incredibly dynamic and multifaceted. We are also wired to organize people and information into simplified buckets because we are constantly processing a tremendous amount of data. This categorization is an essential part of human cognition. Our ability to categorize, however, introduces a rather cruel irony into the mix of being human. The more diverse your experiences, passions, and interests, the more likely you are to feel misunderstood if you haven't yet harnessed the power of your story. This is why these simple exchanges can feel so awkward.

We assume the confusion on the other side is due to our path being chaotic and messy rather than our chaotic and messy explanation of it. But oversimplifying our diverse experiences is equally problematic. One word or a job title can't capture the depth of who we are or the value we provide. The solution lies in connecting the dots along our path—what took us from A to B, all the way to G and beyond. Instead of relying on the other person to connect all those steps, you are going to do it for them.

Recognizing the power of your own story can be challenging at first. You're so close to it that it's easy to write it off as nothing special—just your ordinary life. As you prepare for this exercise, it's essential to remember that your story does have value, and not relative value either. For all our comparisons, each journey is unique; there are no measuring sticks or ranking systems despite what we tell ourselves.

The beauty of a career is that it is an open system. It's not closed off to any environments, and it's in a regular state of flux. While being in a state of flux can have its downside, especially in this current work climate, it also means that:

1. There are multiple ways to reach the same destination
2. There are multiple destinations from the same starting point

Understanding and internalizing this truth is vital as you search for your through lines. It can help you approach your journey with curiosity rather than scrutiny. Connecting the dots in your career is not about judging the stops along the way. It's about acknowledging the whys behind them.

When you own your story, when you trust it, you're not just connecting the dots. You're showing up with presence. You're showing up knowing exactly how point C influenced your arrival at E, and you're not ashamed of or confused by that path. You walked it.

We'll go through two exercises in this next section to help you become an observer of your own story. Think of this as a fact-finding mission to reflect and review your experiences without judgment. If this is your first time doing these exercises, consider this a starting point. You will continue updating your through lines as you encounter new experiences and gather new insights about yourself. But we can start this process with two primary exercises that will serve as your foundation moving forward.

1. **Pattern Finder:** A thorough and repetitive examination of every professional experience you've had to find the recurring themes in each of your working environments.
2. **Lifeline Exercise:** A life inclusive review of your entire life, focusing on the peak and valley experiences that shaped who you are and the decisions you've made.

Finding the Patterns

One of my favorite interview formats is topgrading. This interview methodology focuses on asking questions about a candidate's chronological work history to allow for deeper and more accurate insights into someone's professional history. By asking seemingly repetitive questions about each step of their career, recurring patterns surface that highlight someone's motivators, strengths, and personality traits.

We are going to apply the same approach here, except you are going to be looking for themes and through lines in your career. Stay on the alert for the connective tissue that starts coming to the surface.

Here are the rules:

- This exercise requires two participants, an interviewer and the interviewee (you).
- You want to set aside two hours to ensure there is no time pressure to move faster.
- Recording is recommended so you can go back and grab soundbites. It is also the responsibility of the interviewer to take diligent notes for the interviewee.
- If you attended college, you will start with how you chose your university, how you picked your major, and what you were most proud of during those four years.
- If you did not attend college, you can start with your full-time job.
- If you think you don't have enough work experience to fill two hours, include part-time high school and/or college jobs.
- The interviewer is not allowed to make any assumptions. If you use vague language like "I took the job because I was looking for a new challenge," the interviewer should confirm what you mean by asking, "What do you mean by new challenge?" The gold of this exercise is in the details.
- For EVERY single step of your career (including promotions), the interviewer always asks the same questions:

    1. What led you to take this job?
    2. What are you most proud of?

3. What was your biggest accomplishment?
4. Why did you leave?

Once you talk through a couple of experiences, you will likely start to see patterns emerging—how or why you make decisions, commonalities in the type of work you enjoy the most. Be sure to explore the language you use when discussing what you were most proud of and your biggest accomplishments.

Lifeline Exercise

While the Pattern Finder exercise focuses extensively on our career, this Lifeline Exercise adds more color to the mix by tapping into our broader experiences throughout life that have shaped how we show up.

This exercise was popularized by leadership expert and consultant Doug Conant. In his work with leaders, he found that "many of the problems that leaders face today are the result of their belief that their work life and their 'real' life are two different things. When leaders feel stuck in their career, they often struggle because they have a siloed view of themselves. They have their work identity and their personal identity. And they're at odds. There is no cohesion." Looking at yourself holistically is essential to discovering where you can make the greatest impact.

Carmen Honacker, an international fraud consultant, is well known in her industry as a passionate fighter of cyber-crime and fraud. She originally saw her career in fraud as a happy accident until she reviewed her lifeline; her desire to protect and be a voice for others, she discovered, had been present throughout most of her life.

In third grade, Carmen's teacher asked the class what they wanted to be when they grew up, and Carmen remembered getting in trouble for her response. She had said she wanted to be an angel or Jesus—the only "occupation" she could think of at the time that captured what she truly wanted: having a voice for those who couldn't speak.

As a victim of child of abuse, Carmen knew from a young age that she never wanted someone else to experience what she did. She cared deeply about protecting others, ensuring they were not at a disadvantage, stolen from, or abused. But it wasn't until Carmen reflected on her past through the Lifeline Exercise that she discovered this connection. She thought she had stumbled into a career fighting against cybercrime and fraud when, in reality, she had known she wanted to protect others since she was just eight years old.

Defining moments in our lives serve as data points that can inform how we move forward. They also help us draw meaning from our experiences now that we can look back and see how they connect. Even choices we regret can offer us tremendous value. In his book *The Power of Regret*, Dan Pink shared three key ways that looking backward can help us move forward. Regret, it turns out, has a number of positive upsides. It can:

1. **Improve decision-making.** We can approach future situations differently when we understand

why things didn't work out the first time around.

2. **Boost performance.** Regret causes us to proceed with more caution and consider more alternatives rather than simply jumping into a solution.
3. **Deepen meaning.** When we look at our past experiences through the regret lens of "if only" or "at least," it creates a counterintuitive sense of gratitude for the path we did take.

Now is your chance to look beyond your career and take inventory of all the experiences that played a critical role in shaping your decisions. Set aside time for quiet and uninterrupted reflection. Take a deep breath and try to put aside distractions. On a sheet of paper, draw a grid like the one below.[iii]

LIFELINE EXERCISE

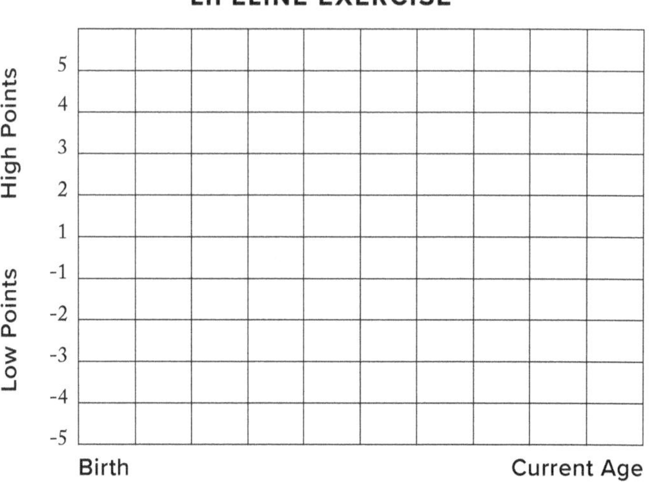

iii You can find a grid worksheet in the Appendix

Next, plot out the major events, achievements, setbacks, social activities/involvements, work experiences, and other experiences that have had a meaningful impact on your life. Place each event at the level of positive or negative impact it had on you (indicated by the distance of each from the horizontal line, representing a neutral effect) and include a few word description for each. As you go through this exercise, trust what comes up for you. This version of your story can be for your eyes only, so there's no need to hold back.

Once you have plotted your points, what stands out to you? Do you recognize any commonalities or language use across your plotted points? These dots are potential stories you can share when telling others about your journey. It's up to you to find those connections and spot which ones played a big part in shaping who you are today.

You can update your narrative moving forward, so there's no need to get it "right" this time around. Doing this exercise the first time requires intensive work, but there's no right or wrong when it comes to self-reflection—only insight.

As we get into Chapter 10, we'll learn how to turn these insights into a narrative that we can share with others. For now, let's turn to another aspect within our control that drastically affects how we show up around others.

Social Power vs. Personal Power

Simply knowing our story doesn't automatically mean we'll

show up with presence. How we narrate that story matters too. Our ability to effectively narrate our story is influenced by our perceived power in a situation. Our sense of power is what allows us to stay open, optimistic, and able to recognize opportunities, especially in situations where we might feel uncomfortable, nervous, or challenged, like meeting someone new, interviewing for a job, or getting outside our comfort zone.

There are two primary types of power: social and personal. Social power, in its simplest form, is power to control others' states and behaviors. Personal power is the ability to control our own states and behaviors.[55]

While ideally we would possess both, personal power is all you need to have presence. Personal power involves tapping into our limitless internal resources—our core values, skills, and authentic selves—when we show up in new spaces. In the next chapter, we'll get into how you can begin tapping into this personal power.

EIGHT

Building Your Foundation

"Knowing yourself is not a destination; it's a practice."

—Tara Brach

It was the summer of 2015 and Jen Rittenhouse had just done the unthinkable. She had just turned down her dream job—the one she spent twenty years working toward.

The inkling that something was misaligned started surfacing at the end of 2014, when Jen was changing out the family calendar. This wasn't just any calendar. This was the master calendar, the command center, with all the family's activities and growing demands. At the time, both Jen and her husband had senior leadership positions that required frequent travel. Their preteen kids were involved in multiple activities, adding to the complexity.

In a moment of nostalgia, Jen began flipping through the old calendar. As she got further into the year, she couldn't help noticing that she and her husband had traveled more than she realized. At a glance, they looked like two ships passing in the night. Intrigued, Jen decided to count the amount of time they had been home at the same time, and she was shocked by what she discovered. They had only been home together for seven of the fifty-two weeks that year. She had known things seemed a bit crazy, but she had no idea it was this severe.

As the new year began, Jen started noticing a growing desire to be more present with her daughters. They were entering their teen years and seemed to need her presence more than ever before. Jen's intuitive voice got louder as she began sensing a shift in her priorities. But the usual distractions of their fast-paced work and home life made it too easy to ignore. Then things started to take a turn for the worse at work. The company was struggling to make their numbers, and by the summer, Jen found herself in a position she never expected or experienced before. Laid off and unemployed.

Jen immediately jumped into action mode, reaching out to her network, polishing her resume, and making new connections, even landing a few initial interviews. All the while, her intuition kept speaking. While she had initially felt shock at being laid off, she had also felt relief, as though a weight had been lifted off her shoulders. With her schedule open, she spent more time with her daughters, and it quickly became clear to Jen that this was where she wanted to prioritize her time. Whatever she did next, it would need to give her the flexibility of being home with her family and attending her kids' activities.

It wasn't long before Jen was entering the final interview process for an executive HR position with a major US company. In many ways, this role was the culmination of everything she had worked toward—a significant bump in compensation and a C-level title. Except there was a major hangup; since this was a global executive role, Jen would be expected to travel 70-80% of the time. She would get to do that travel on the company's private jet, but at the cost of time with family. If she accepted the role, she would be signing up for the exact thing she was aiming to change. She saw it all clearly, and she didn't want it.

The hiring manager sat in stunned silence as Jen politely declined. To many, this would have been an incredibly attractive offer, maybe an irresistible one. But Jen knew that no title or amount of money could compensate for her presence at home, at least not in this chapter of her life.

Throughout this process, Jen had been reflecting on what she wanted. She knew she still wanted to pursue her career, and that she was still deeply passionate about HR. She also knew she wanted flexibility in her schedule, minimal travel, and an environment where she could grow. As she looked at her next chapter through this lens, she was reminded of something. Over the course of her career, there were several local small and medium size companies who often needed her expertise but didn't have the budget or need to hire someone with her credentials full time. That's when she knew her next steps. Rather than continue searching for positions within a company, she launched an HR consulting practice for small and medium size companies.

There was still one thing she hadn't figured out though. How could she create a growth environment for herself? Once again, the answer presented itself through reflection. Jen had long been familiar with the University of Tennessee; it was practically in her backyard and her previous employers would frequently recruit new graduates. Jen decided to pursue a PhD in Business Administration and Management, eventually becoming a regular lecturer at the Haslam College of Business Honors Experience. Not only did she grow, she was now able to share her passion for HR with the future leaders of business.

For the first time in years, Jen had given herself space to do the internal work needed to understand what was most important to her at this stage of her life and career. While walking away from the executive position seemed like a huge risk, that decision created space for her to design a career that aligned with her shifting priorities.

Imagine if Jen had not spontaneously decided to flip through the calendar and count the amount of time their family was at home together. How much longer might she have continued down the path, knowing it wasn't quite right and growing further misaligned with her intuition, despite having what society deemed valuable? How many of us default to what we know rather than designing a life based on what we want? It's unnerving how easily this can happen.

Feminist philosopher Katie Mann describes a system in which there are two primary roles: human givers and human beings. Human beings are allowed, even expected, to embrace their full humanity. Human givers, on the other hand, are expected to offer their time and energy in support of others' needs. For human givers, articulating what they want is a violation of their role and fuels the belief that self-focus is selfishness.

As women, we're imprinted with gender norms without our permission or consent; we're conditioned to be human givers. It's no wonder we find ourselves further disconnected from our sense of self as life grows in complexity with work, family, and social commitments—we were never connected to begin with. It wasn't okay to be both a woman and a human being.

Now that we know the conditions working against us, we can rebuild—or perhaps build for the first time—our sense of self. Our foundation.

Building Your Foundation

Building your personal foundation is important, as it will serve as your alignment compass moving forward—something you can reference to determine if you're heading in the direction you want to go, not just moving forward on autopilot. This process is most effective when we're vulnerable and honest and have the courage to ask ourselves the hard questions. You've likely done aspects of this work over the years whether you realize it or not, but we're going to walk through the following four core components of an internal foundation together:

1. Priority Dimension
2. Core Values
3. Energy Givers/Takers
4. Claiming Your Unique Skills and Superpowers (so important that it gets its own chapter after this one)

Ground Rules

Before we get into the work there are a few important ground rules we need to discuss. These might seem obvious, but they're helpful reminders we all deserve, especially when society often tells us the opposite.

1. **Shed the shoulds.** As you go through the next two chapters, consider them a "should free" zone. In my experience, the "shoulds" usually arise when what we want is in conflict with what we believe others think we should want. This is about YOU, so those external opinions can just see their way out.

2. **Be real, not aspirational.** It can be tempting to answer questions based on what you aspire to be rather than who you are. If you are finding this difficult, I'll share a saying my mother always used to say to me: "You are unique. In all the history of the world there was never anyone exactly like you, and in all the infinity to come there will never be another YOU."
3. **There is no good/bad or right/wrong.** This might be your first devoted time to really begin tuning in to yourself and what you want. Be kind, be patient, and trust what's coming up. If it feels hard, it's ok to step away for a day. If your intuition tells you something you don't like, sit with that. It's natural to resist change, even the good kind. The key is to honor yourself and what you feel throughout this process.
4. **Think like a scientist.** Our ability to rethink and unlearn is arguably the most valuable skill we possess in this ever-changing world. In his book *Think Again*, Adam Grant describes four professional mindsets we bring to the table when thinking or talking: Preacher, Prosecutor, Politician, and Scientist. The preacher inspires and sways, the prosecutor levels you with facts to convince you they're right, and the politician becomes whatever is most favorable to them. With a scientist mindset, "you're expected to doubt what you know, be curious

about what you don't know, and update your views based on new data." In other words, a scientist is not judgmental but curious, and I encourage you to adopt this mindset as you build your foundation. Seek first to understand. Stay curious about yourself. And approach what you discover with fascination.

5. **Change is the only constant.** Your core values will serve as your guiding compass, but other components of your life, desires, and needs will evolve with time. You have full permission to change your mind as you have new experiences, enter a new phase of life, or experience a shift in your priorities. What matters to you now will likely be different in a few years. This is not a cause for concern. It is a signal of growth.

Now that we are on the same page, let's get into the work.

Priority Dimension

Building our foundation starts with understanding which dimension of life is currently your priority. There are six primary dimensions in our lives: relationship, personal, community, financial, professional, and spiritual.

Equipped with an understanding of her priority dimension, Jen was able to make one of the biggest decisions in her career with clarity. She knew what season of life she was in, what dimension she was channeling her energy toward, and how that influenced her day-to-day actions.

Because of that self-knowledge, she was able to make an informed decision about what to say no (and yes) to.

Looking at this list, you might already have clarity on your priority dimension or, alternatively, you might be struggling to choose just one. Regardless of your level of clarity, the following questions will take you deeper into self-reflection on each dimension.

Relationship

- What is your ideal relationship like? What kind of partner do you want to be in an intimate relationship?
- How do you want to interact with your family members?
- What type of parent do you want to be? How do you want to interact with your children?
- Why is friendship important to you? What type of friend do you want to be? How would you behave toward your best friend?

Personal

- Is learning important to you? Are there any skills you'd like to learn?
- What type of recreational activities do you enjoy? What type of activities would you really like to engage in? Why do you enjoy those activities?
- What issues related to health and physical well-being do you care about (e.g. sleep, diet, exercise)? Why and how do you take care of yourself?

Community

- Are community activities (volunteering, voting, recycling, etc.) important to you? Why?
- What community activities are you drawn toward?
- Are there other social, political, or professional networks and groups you would like to participate in?

Financial

- What financial resources do you require to support your current lifestyle?
- What financial resources do you require to support your desired lifestyle?
- Are there any long-term needs or wants?

Professional

- What do you value about your work? (Ex. Intellectual challenge? Independence? Prestige? Interacting with people? Helping others?)
- What type of work would you like to do?
- What does your ideal professional day look like?

Spiritual

- What is your north star? Why do you do what you do?
- What do you hold on to during difficult times?

Now that you've taken time to better understand what matters to you across these six dimensions, you likely have a stronger sense for which dimension is your current priority. Does anything surprise you? Do you agree with the dimension that seems to be your highest priority? Are you experiencing a shift in your priorities?

For the second dimension exercise, we'll create a visual that helps us spot where there might be misalignment in our lives. Using the Alignment Worksheet, you will rate two things for each dimension: importance and satisfaction.

1. **Importance.** How much of a priority is this dimension? Assign a value between 1-3; one being a low priority and three being the highest. Keep in mind that you want one, max two dimensions rated a three.
2. **Time.** When you look at your calendar, is it easy to see you're spending time in this dimension? You will do the same exercise but this time you will assign a value between 1-3 based on time spent per dimension. One means little to no time spent on the dimension and three means a lot of time.

Again, just like the questions you answered earlier, this exercise is not about shoulds. It's about honoring what is most important to you in this season of life. If you get stuck, refer back to your dimension questions. Your calendar can also help you identify where you're spending time. If you're a numbers person, consider throwing the data into a spreadsheet to create a graph that visually shows you a ratio of how much time you spend in each dimension. Remember, there's no right or wrong way to do this exercise. You do you.

Alignment Worksheet

Importance	**SPIRITUAL**	Time
1 2 3		1 2 3
Importance	**PERSONAL**	Time
1 2 3		1 2 3
Importance	**PROFESSIONAL**	Time
1 2 3		1 2 3
Importance	**RELATIONAL**	Time
1 2 3		1 2 3
Importance	**COMMUNITY**	Time
1 2 3		1 2 3
Importance	**FINANCIAL**	Time
1 2 3		1 2 3

Once you complete this exercise, you will have two insights: which dimension is your top priority, and whether or not you're currently misaligned. Misalignment will show up as having a high priority but a low satisfaction in a particular dimension or, conversely, a low priority but a high satisfaction in a particular dimension.

You've officially begun building your foundation. Knowing what dimension is most important to you can serve as a compass when you're faced with small and big decisions alike. Your priorities give you permission to say no without FOMO or get you back on track when you sense yourself being stretched too thin. You can always come back to this alignment exercise whenever you need to reground yourself; your foundation will be there.

Energy Givers and Takers

Tina was an enterprise software sales professional who came to me expressing a frustration with tech and sales. She was convinced that she did not operate well in the type of environment her job required, despite being extremely successful. As we went through her pattern finder exercise, we spotted a common theme; starting with her jobs in high school, Tina thrived in ambiguous environments where her input was valued and where she was given autonomy to figure out creative solutions. Once we got to her most recent role, we could pinpoint when things shifted from energy giving to energy taking.

Starting out, Tina was one of the first reps at a growing

tech startup. She found a sales process that produced great results, and her teammates sought her out for tips and coaching. After a few years and significant company growth, a new Chief Revenue Officer arrived on the scene. He began implementing his sales process and demanded that all the reps use it. Tina was frustrated that as a top performer she was never consulted about her process, and now she was being forced to use a process that had not been proven to be more effective. She realized through our work together that selling was not the issue—changes to the environment were in conflict with how she operated best. She had been ready to walk away from a career, all because she had misidentified the root issue.

Consider your pattern finder exercise. Were there any patterns you identified that impacted your energy, either positively or negatively? Make a note of those somewhere that's easy to reference later.

Exercise #1: The To-Do List

We are going to use your to-do list for the first exercise. If you do not use a to-do list or yours is only a professional list, then take a moment now to make a list of everything on your life to-do list. This should be inclusive of all life dimensions. Now that you have your list, go through it and ask yourself:

- What on this list am I looking forward to?
- What am I dreading?
- What am I neutral or indifferent toward?

Once you've marked each item on your list accordingly, look again at the things you're dreading. Go through each one and ask yourself what it is about that task you are dreading. Don't settle for simple answers; keep asking yourself why until you get to a root cause. After you have gone through all of them, look for emerging patterns, for example:

- Are there certain phrases or words that come up?
- Is there a similar environment across these dreaded to-dos?
- Are there specific people involved?

Jot down any patterns you see, then repeat the same exercise with the items you're looking forward to.

Exercise #2: Gathering Additional Data

Now that your mind is primed to think about your energy levels, observe your energy over the coming week. Here are questions to consider as you do so:

Energy Takers

- What makes me feel tired when I think about doing it?
- What leaves me feeling drained and unfulfilled after I do it?
- What gives me a knot in my stomach when I think about doing it?

Energy Givers

- What do I look forward to doing?

- What activities made me happy?
- What activities made me lose track of time?
- I love when people ask for my help with…

After you do this exercise, you'll have a rich set of data that you can review and mine through for helpful insights on how you operate best.

What if energy takers can't be avoided?

The reality is that there will always be energy-taking components in our lives. Even with this work, there are still things you'll need to do as part of your job, your life responsibilities, or simply activities that are important to you but still drain you. That is okay. The pivotal part of this exercise is becoming aware of what gives you energy and what takes it away.

Whether you're choosing to do something hard—for personal growth or to serve a higher purpose—or whether you're in an exhausting job that you can't afford to quit, the key is finding ways to manage your energy. Knowing your energy givers and takers allows you to begin making adjustments.

NINE

Exploration

> "I have learned that as long as I hold fast to my beliefs and values, and follow my own moral compass, then the only expectations I need to live up to are my own."
>
> —Michelle Obama

Core values anchor us to our most authentic selves when we face important decisions or proverbial forks in the road. They keep us grounded when people with good intentions (or bad ones) try to pull us off our path.

While many of us understand the importance of having personal values, the creation of personal values is still an elusive process. A frequent question I hear whether I'm facilitating my foundation building workshop or working with a new client is, "How do you even begin to define core values?" The answer is turning to the data within our own lives.

Our emotions are a powerful source of data. In particular, strong negative emotions often signal that a value is getting stepped on. The challenge is that we are indoctrinated into a culture that encourages us to push away these valuable insights in the pursuit of happiness and positivity.[56] But this pervasive insistence on positive thinking leads to avoidance, suppression, or flat out denial of our own emotions. We are inundated with life hacking tips that promise a quick fix to improve things we don't enjoy so we don't have to feel bad or uncomfortable. We are encouraged to avoid our feelings rather than lean into them.

The irony is that the greatest insights come when we can sit in our discomfort. Dr. Susan David is a renowned psychologist who has studied emotions, happiness, and achievement for two decades. Through her extensive research, she found that it was not intelligence or even creativity that fueled success but rather emotional agility, particularly in an uncertain world. She defines emotional agility as the practice of using our feelings as information to guide us rather than trying to change or control them.

When we can approach our emotions with curiosity rather than judgment, they become a valuable tool in bringing our best selves forward. Negative emotions in particular, David notes, are "beacons, not barriers, helping us identify what we most care about." In other words, negative emotions are powerful signposts of our values.

Now that you understand the connection between emotions and core values, let's walk through four steps to create a first draft (or an updated draft if you've done a similar exercise before) of your personal core values.

Step 1: Gather the Data

Diagnosing situations that elicit strong negative emotions, also known as valley experiences, is an effective starting point to begin building your values. Over the next couple of weeks, you're going to document your valley experiences. You can do this in a journal, a document on your computer, or anywhere that works best for you.

The important thing is taking detailed notes while the incident is still fresh in your mind. Be sure to observe and include a variety of interactions (familial, professional, romantic, community, etc.). This will ensure you have a rich set of data to pull from later. Try to capture at least seven or more experiences before moving on to step two. Remember, the more data you have, the better your future insights.

For each valley experience, answer the following questions:

- What happened?
- Where were you?
- Who was with you?
- What was going on?
- What were you feeling? How did your body feel?

Step 2: Collect Quantity, Not Quality

Once you have a collection of experiences that elicited strong negative emotions, you're going to inspect those experiences and go down a few layers to identify the potential values that were getting stepped on.

As you begin exploring potential core values associated with your valley experiences, there are a few important things to keep in mind:

- Values are chosen, not imposed. You create your values.
- Values are not aspirational, they are lived in our day-to-day lives, whether we recognize their influence or not.
- They are personal. What works for you won't be the same as what works for another person.

Come back to these reminders any time you need a quick refresh or sense yourself growing judgmental. The key is knowing there are no good or bad values. There is simply what is important to you.

There are two important steps to reviewing your valley experiences. The first is to identify the root cause of your emotion. (A way to ensure you get below the surface is to keep asking yourself "Why?" until you can't answer any further.) The second is to assign potential core values to each experience. This is not a time to be overly discerning; you are going for quantity over quality in this second step.[iv] We will focus on refinement later. Then you will repeat this process for each of your valley experiences, first identifying

---

iv There is a sample list of values and definitions in the Appendix

the root cause, then assigning a potential value.

Let's look at a couple of examples to help you get a sense of what digging beneath the surface of your valley experiences might look like.

One of my coaching clients shared that one of her valley experiences happened on a zoom call with other managers. Her peer made a snide comment putting down a team that worked closely with their group. This elicited smiles and smirks from others on the call, and although she did not agree with this comment she stayed silent. In this experience, there were two parts to examine deeper: the comment itself, and the fact that she stayed silent.

When I asked her why she was upset by the comment, she shared that, because this was a team they worked closely with, it seemed wrong to speak about them behind their back without telling them there was an issue. Then I asked why it bothered her that the issue had not been brought to the team's attention. She was frustrated that this behavior was just accepted by the company, she said. Rather than solve problems, they were pointing fingers. We kept digging deeper, and when I asked her why it bothered her that the default was finger pointing, she asked a question of her own: "If there is no communication then how is a team supposed to make adjustments? You continue solving the wrong problem and operating inefficiently." It was clear to both of us that she was passionate about working together to tackle meaningful problems—not just get through them with the same issues at play.

As we continued digging into this valley experience, she recognized several potential values that were getting stepped on, including respect, communication, collaboration, and responsibility. By isolating the incident that triggered the emotion, we were able to uncover the reasons she had been upset, and consequently name a few of her core values.

Let's take a look at another example, this time in the relationship dimension. Emma was a marketing executive and a mother of two preteens. Emma's valley experience came one night while getting dinner ready for the family. Emma was admittedly exhausted from a long day and felt herself growing increasingly angry as her two kids screwed around instead of doing the chore she had just asked them to do. Feeling ignored yet again, Emma yelled at the kids to stop messing around and do what she had told them.

Emma was immediately horrified at how quickly and intensely she responded to the situation. For her values, she told me she wanted to be more patient, supportive, and caring. I think you know what comes next. After gently reminding Emma that core values are not aspirational, I asked her what about the kids not listening had upset her.

She exhaled deeply. "I've been so exhausted lately," she began. "When this happened, my husband was watching TV and I felt like I was juggling multiple things at once—trying to get dinner ready, trying to corral the kids—after what had already been a long day." She didn't like how she communicated with her kids, though, because their behavior didn't justify her reaction.

Now we were getting somewhere. Since this valley experience seemed to stem from exhaustion, I pushed a little deeper to understand why she was so exhausted. "People in my life just assume I can take things on," Emma shared. She had gotten a few unexpected requests at work without a follow-up conversation at home about what would need to be taken off her priority list to accommodate the added work load. She was annoyed with her husband in that moment because he was getting to relax while she was running around trying to do everything. Her anger toward the kids actually had nothing to do with what was really bothering her. It was merely a symptom of her real anger, which was the absence of reciprocity and respect from her husband regarding her and her time. There it was. Emma had identified the possible values getting stepped on: reciprocity, trust, and respect.

Like Emma, you may find that the original valley experience may not be the true source of your strong emotion. By continuing to stay curious about what occurred, you can hone in on the true root cause.

Step 3: Create Your Clusters

For this next step, you want to reference all of your potential values in one location, whether that's on a spreadsheet, a scrap of paper, or a blank document. You are looking for two things as you assess this list. The first is the frequency of recurring values. To make this easier, highlight or circle the recurring values in your document so they visually stand out. The second thing you are looking for are the themes among these values. You will group these values under related themes. For example, you might notice you have values with similar definitions on your sheet. For the sake of the example, let's say you have responsibility, order and stability.

- Responsibility: to be responsible and accountable for my actions
- Order: to be orderly and organized
- Stability: to prioritize a sense of balance, consistency, and predictability

Once you have your value clusters, look for the central theme of each cluster, maybe even circling the word that best represents it. Using the same example from above, you notice that this cluster of values all convey a sense of reliability. You can write your own definition for the value which might be:

Reliability: to be trustworthy due to a consistent, organized, and predictable presence

After this refinement process, you may still have a sizable list of values. While the number of core values differs for each person, the magic range to aim for is between five to seven values. Too many, and you risk forgetting them or being so inclusive of what counts as a value that they become ineffective guides. You want your values to be an effective compass, not a compass with multiple needles pointing in all directions. If you're struggling to whittle down your list, ask yourself these questions:

- Which of these values are essential to my life?
- Which of these values represent my primary way of being?
- Which of these values are essential to supporting my inner self?

Using your answers, go back and rank your values in order of importance and consider eliminating the lowest ranking value(s). You could also do another round of clustering your values to help you consolidate them into a similar, overarching value.

At the end of the day, you are creating this list of core values to test them out in the coming weeks and months and see if they continue resonating as true for you. If you don't feel ready to move into this testing phase, you can continue writing down valley experiences to gather additional data to inform your values.

Step 4: Define Your Values

The final step of defining your core values is writing down a description for each one. You can use a dictionary definition or craft a more personal version based on what that value means to you.

Keep in mind that these steps simply aim to get you to a first draft of your personal values. You can always make adjustments and refine this list as you continue gaining new insights about yourself.

With the final piece of your foundation in place, it's time to move into the next step of the process: the activation phase.

TEN

Activation

"Success is rarely a solo act."

—Indra Nooyi

Until this point in the book, you've been able to do most of the work on your own. While it has been hard work learning about the various factors influencing our careers and clarifying what we want to take with us through our career transition, it has also been safe. You could still turn back and no one would be the wiser that you were exploring a change. But continuing on this journey means you will need to engage others and ask for their support. In short, you will need to network.

There is a good chance you just scoffed at that last sentence, and you wouldn't be alone in doing so. Beyond the fact that we're raised on the myth of meritocracy, research has found that women view networking very differently than their male counterparts. When asked about their recent promotions, 77% of women believed it was the result of their credentials and hard work as compared to their male counterparts, 83% of whom believed their promotion was the result of their network.[57]

When you hear the word "networking," what is the first thought that comes to mind? Do you shiver a little thinking about the awkward small talk you have to endure? Or do you feel icky because the process seems so superficial and disingenuous? Maybe you dread talking about yourself. What do you even say? The way networking has been represented historically contradicts the way women typically engage, so it's no wonder the idea of it elicits such strong reactions.

The aversion or de-prioritization of networking becomes even more prevalent as women approach mid-career. Research shows that the gap between men and women networking widens after age thirty-five, where only a quarter of women network at least once a week compared to nearly half of men. This disparity grows more significant after kids get added to the mix, where less than 25% of mothers say they network more than once a week compared to just over 50% of fathers.

In her 2010 report "The Sponsor Effect: Breaking Through The Glass Ceiling," economist and professor Sylvia Ann Hewlett identified that although women were happy to ask for business favors on behalf of others, they had a strong aversion to asking on their own behalf. Despite having more close friends than men, women are less likely to use these relationships for career advancement and have a tendency to avoid mixing business and pleasure.

Because women are socialized to be attentive to others' needs over our own, expressing discontent with our current situation, making an ask of our network, even prioritizing our needs ahead of the team or company can feel both unnatural and uncomfortable. Too often, this normal disconnect can lead women to avoid networking altogether.

On the surface, it appears that the numbers are (once again) not in women's favor. Statistically, networking is still the highest driver for landing our next role. Some industry experts have estimated that 70% of open positions are never even posted.[v] Unlike men's experiences with promotion, however, the size of a woman's network does not necessarily lead to professional advancement.[58] The reality is that women don't network like men and they shouldn't. What works for men is often not the same as what works for women. Rather than unfairly expecting ourselves to change, let's aim to better understand how we network (or don't network), why this approach differs, and how we can view networking moving forward.

Consider how it feels when someone seeks your

---

v The research on this data is controversial. Through my research of female careers, I found that 68% landed roles through people they knew. This was being recruited or tapping their network for support.

guidance or help. If you derive joy from helping others and from others valuing your perspective, chances are you don't mind that they reached out to you for help—in fact, you might even be glad they did. When you reach out to someone for their help with your career, aren't you giving that same gift to someone else? (Spoiler alert: you are!)

Maybe that's not your hangup though. Maybe you feel selfish asking someone for their time when you don't have something equivalent you can do for them. But what if you reframe that feeling of selfishness? What if the truly selfish act is withholding your talents and gifts from the world?

Filling in the Missing Pieces

Even when you get past the resistance to network, you'll likely encounter a new set of questions or concerns when enlisting others' help. It is normal to get to this stage of the process and still have no idea what you want to do. While you have made tremendous progress, you are still in full-blown liminal state. But that doesn't mean you can't reach out to others. In fact, quite the opposite. When you feel murky or unclear, your network can lend some of its greatest value.

Jenn Goldstone was a news producer at ABC who had spent the last twelve years rising through the ranks. She loved the work, but her growing desire to start a family was becoming more and more important. As much as she wanted to believe motherhood wouldn't change her career trajectory, she had watched too many powerhouse female journalists become mothers themselves and get sidelined from the best stories as a result. Facing the painful reality of what being a mother meant in this industry, Jenn made the choice to explore alternatives.

Rather than trying to solve the entire situation all at once, Jenn started by asking herself, "What skills do I have? What am I doing at work when I am my happiest? What am I doing when I am in flow?" She was most in flow, she realized, when she was talking with people, storytelling, and building relationships. She then began listing her strengths, skills, and personal mission, assessing the dimensions outside of her professional life as well. Once she was finished, she shared this list with her husband, who noted that her skills resembled the skills of the woman in charge of fundraising at his alma mater.

His response surprised Jenn. She knew this line of work existed, but she'd never considered pursuing it herself. With her curiosity piqued, she leveraged her investigative journalist skills and set out doing research. Jenn connected with a woman from her husband's alma mater to learn about what the role entailed, and she read several books on the topic too. She determined this line of work was indeed something she would enjoy and something that would be a great transfer of her skill set.

Now that Jenn had narrowed down her focus, her next steps were easier to see. She went back to her network, this time with a more specific request: connecting with foundations that had open positions. Through her network, she eventually got connected with a hiring manager at Outward Bound. As fate would have it, the hiring manager had a brother who was a journalist and knew what an asset it would be to have a journalist's skill set on board. That, combined with how Jenn presented her prior work experience in the context of this new world, made the offer an easy yes. Jenn was hired as the National Director of Foundation Relations. This transition launched her into an incredibly successful career in nonprofits. Jenn eventually became COO for Birthright Israel Foundation, the largest educational tourism organization in the United States, gifting over 50,000 young Jewish adults with educational trips to Israel each year.

Jenn started into her career transition with the belief that there was, indeed, a valuable use for her unique experience. By turning to her trusted advisors and networking, she was able to crowdsource ideas for alternate career paths and ultimately land her next career opportunity.

Career Networking Document

One of my favorite resources to use at this stage is what I call the Career Networking Document. This document helps you organize your newly discovered insights from your foundation work in a format that you can easily share with others to begin gathering feedback. There are six key components to this document: a professional objective, your branding statement, your skills/competencies, key accomplishments, target market attributes, and finally your target sector and organization. Let's go through each of these in more detail.

Professional Objective: This describes the impact you want or intend to make in your next professional move. Think of this as similar to a vision statement, and keep it between 1-2 sentences.

Branding Statement: Write a high-level summary of your personal brand, including 2-3 sentences about what you bring to a team/company/environment. If you are considering a career change, you can also include where you're headed next (this can be high level, such as "I'm planning to transition into the social impact sector).

Skills/Competencies: Think of this as a keyword list for your primary skills (ex. negotiations, M&A) and the technology/platforms you've used (PowerBI, Salesforce).

Key Accomplishments: In this section, highlight accomplishments throughout your career that best support your next step. If you don't yet know what you're looking for, then focus on the accomplishments that made you feel most alive and aligned. Aim for 5-7 bullets. Make sure to provide any context that helps portray the significance of the work.

Target Market Attributes: Here is where you get more

specific about where you want to work. This includes specific industries, company cultures and/or values, and location.

Target Sector & Organization: Depending on what you uncovered in your exploration phase, this section may be difficult to fill out initially. It's perfectly fine to update this section as you gain more insights into the type of work you want to do or the specific organizations/employers on your wishlist.

Filling out this document will help you practice describing yourself, your skills, and what opportunities you're seeking next. It's designed to help you take the incredible insights you gained in your exploration phase into your next action steps. In addition to being a resource to share with others, it can also help you formulate your elevator pitch. If you want to make your transition more public facing, then your branding statement can double as a LinkedIn summary as well.

Your Career Crew

Now that you have your Career Networking Document started, let's talk about the three key archetypes you can leverage in this exploration process: mentor, sponsor, and coach.

Mentors are individuals who can serve as experienced and trusted advisors. These individuals can be coworkers or even a boss, but they don't have to be. The nature of this relationship can ebb and flow, fluctuating from active to inactive depending on your current focus and needs.

Sponsors are leaders or individuals who hold power and influence within your company. These are strategic relationships to establish when you're looking to advance. Think of a sponsor like an extension of yourself. They are present in rooms where ideas get discussed and decisions are made that you're not privy to, and they can serve as an advocate or champion for you and your work.

Coaches are paid professionals to help you achieve mutually agreed upon goals. While there are no rules around when to work with a coach, this relationship is best leveraged during times of transition or high growth—whenever you're considering a change or learning new skills.

As you look at this list, who comes to mind as part of your career crew? Can you think of two, maybe three people that you can reach out to? Follow that intuition as a good starting point. You can add more people to your list as you go, but begin networking with your current contacts by sending them a simple note like the one below:

> *Subject Line: Time to Connect?*
>
> *Hi {Name},*
>
> *I have been exploring some possible career moves and I would love to get your perspective as someone whose opinion I value. I have attached a career networking document that I would love to walk through together when we meet.*

> *Are you available this week or next to grab coffee (or however you typically meet)?*
>
> *With joy,*
>
> *{Your signoff}*

If you're scheduling preliminary conversations, the next questions starting to surface might be:

- What should I say? I'm not even sure what I want yet.
- I don't want to waste their time. How do I maximize this interaction?
- How do I figure out if they can help me or not?

If you are knee deep in liminality with zero idea what to do next, then use this time with your contacts to brainstorm possible career ideas based on your objective, branding statement, skills, and accomplishments. You can use the ideas you come up with together as a starting point for further exploration later. Some starter questions might be:

- What roles might align with my skills and experiences?
- Are there any organizations I should look into based on my purpose and branding statement?
- Is there someone you recommend I connect with?

If you already have a strong idea of possible careers you want to target, then focus your conversation on companies, people, or organizations they might know that you should look into. Depending on what or who they recommend, see if your contact is comfortable making a direct intro on your behalf. This might feel like too much to ask—it isn't. They can always say no to your request; but if you don't ask, the answer's always no. So stick your neck out there. The risk is worth it.

Create a few versions of a forwardable intro.

Before you cringe at the thought of doing this I want you to consider if someone you cared about came to you and asked you to write a description of what makes them awesome. My guess is that you would not think twice about singing their praises. Treat your career networking document as though it is this awesome person you care about. Write it as though you are writing about this other person, not yourself. Honor that individual and all that they have accomplished.

Example:

Sarah is a dynamic human who has lived many career lives including collegiate basketball coach and customer service leader for scaling tech companies. Through her breadth of experience she is adept at cutting through noise to quickly understand a situation, gathering data to inform opportunities for optimization. As far as she is concerned the gnarlier the challenge the better. Alex is exploring product management as the next move in her career and is looking to connect with industry experts to learn more about how to position her skills and experience for these types of roles.

Build and Test

Now that you've engaged a few of your trusted crew, you are beginning the transition from activation to Build and Test. The goal of this phase is testing out several career hypotheses, each time gathering new insights and data to help you understand yourself deeper and illuminate your best next step.

Feedback is an integral part of this process, but not all feedback is equal. Discerning what feedback to receive and which feedback to filter out is paramount in staying true to yourself.

No one knows this better than Tiffany Castagno. After nearly thirteen years working in medical and then legal billing, Tiffany was making a major career change. She viewed her previous work experience as irrelevant to her future career aspirations, and so she set out to earn a Master's in HR and labor relations. As Tiffany began interviewing for HR positions, she kept getting the same pushback from hiring managers who saw her education but questioned her lack of "real world experience."

Tiffany interviewed at the last company she had applied to, feeling defeated and questioning herself. This time, however, something different happened as Tiffany talked about her past. The hiring manager connected the dots between Tiffany's prior experience and the skills needed in this new role. She got a callback. After several more interviews, Tiffany was hired into her first HR position. Her new manager would also become her first mentor, playing a vital role in helping Tiffany understand and articulate the value of her story.

Both internal and external mentors offer benefits and present potential challenges when making a career transition. An internal mentor can be helpful because they know the players, culture, and unspoken rules that exist within the field or company you're already in. They understand certain dynamics within the work environment that may be difficult for someone to recognize from the outside. The downside is that, because they're already in the same bubble as you, they may hold a similar view of the world—an in-group perspective—when you need perspective from the outside. That's where external mentors come in.

External mentors help you to step outside your workspace bubble and provide a safe space for vulnerable dialogue about your field or company. They don't have to juggle you alongside the company agenda. They're available for whatever issues you need to discuss as part of your potential transition. This positioning is known as the out-group advantage.

An in-group is a group of people unified by a shared identity, belief, or trait. For example, individuals working on the same team or at the same company form an in-group, whether it's intentional or not. An out-group is anyone who's different from those in the in-group. While humans seek out those who hold similar opinions, research has found that "socially different group members do more than simply introduce new viewpoints or approaches. Diverse groups outperformed more homogeneous groups not because of an influx of new ideas, but because diversity triggered more careful information processing that is absent in homogeneous groups."[59]

who do you trust?

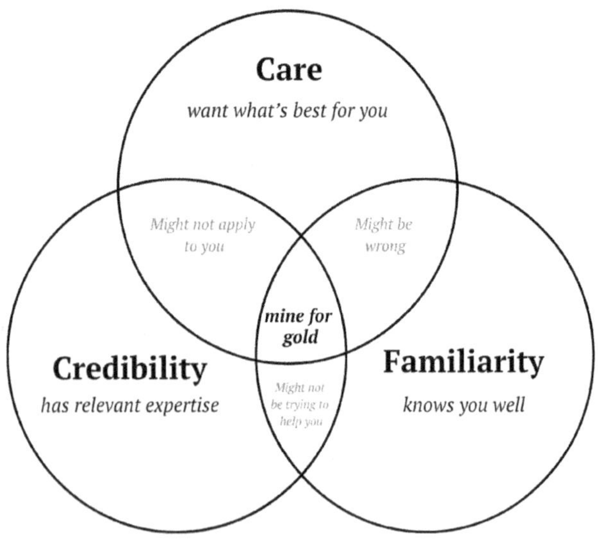

Source: Grant, Adam. Hidden Potential. 2023. Viking

For this very reason, it's important to get the perspective of both your internal and external mentors when making a career move. But regardless of their connection to you and your current role/company, they must be trustworthy. You are inviting their feedback in a vulnerable time of transition. How do you know whether or not to trust your mentors, sponsors, or coach?

In his book *Hidden Potential*, Adam Grant breaks down trustworthiness into three components: care, credibility, and familiarity.[vi]

As you approach each conversation with your career crew, consider these three elements and ask yourself the following questions:

1. Do they care about me as a person?
2. Do they know me? Not just who I am now but who I am becoming?
3. Do they have relevant expertise in the areas we're discussing?

You don't have to answer yes to all three of these questions in order for someone to be considered trustworthy, but you need to stay aware of these dynamics when seeking out feedback. Be careful of giving credence to someone who hasn't repeatedly earned your trust by caring about you or who hasn't demonstrated their credibility and familiarity with the move you want to make or the process

---

vi Source: Hidden Potential by Adam Grant

you're going through.

Psychologists have found that when you're new to a skill, asking for advice is not always helpful. It's too early to get feedback, because you don't even know your own limits. As you acquire some experience, however, you gain more confidence and your focus shifts from finding affirmation of that new skill to finding information to improve on what you're learning.[60] You can actually evaluate and implement the advice you're given.

In conversations with your network, listen for phrases like "I think that..." or "If I were you..." or "I feel like..." These phrases often signal that someone is giving you their personal opinion as opposed to lending insight based on experience. When you hear someone start a sentence that way, follow it up with something like, "That's really interesting. What makes you say that?" Often, their answer to this question will illuminate if their comment or observation was just a thought or something based on valid experience.

In addition to involving your trusted support in this activation phase, throw your net a little wider. When making a career change, it turns out that our existing connections are not usually the most helpful. Career reinvention expert Herminia Ibarra refers to two additional ways of building relationships that enable career change: Bridge and Bond.[61] Bridge refers to creating or reactivating relationships beyond your current social and professional circle. This expands your current circles and increases your access to new information and opportunities. (Hint: you're already doing this when you ask your existing contacts for introductions to their network.)

Bond is about deepening ties and finding community with a close circle of kindred spirits. These bonding relationships are particularly helpful as you navigate the uncertainty of transition. They offer support and space to process emotions and information during this phase. These bonding relationships can be with people you already know, such as your spouse and friend circle, or they can be with others going through a career transition themselves, or you can find them in the field where you're wanting to work. The important thing is forming that bond and surrounding yourself with trustworthy individuals, no matter where you find them.

While this journey is ultimately about you, who you surround yourself with plays an important role in your experience.

ELEVEN

Commit

"Risk doesn't have to mean recklessness. It can mean thoughtful experimentation."

—Julia Boorstin

Women's appetite for risk has largely been misunderstood. The popular narrative is that women are risk averse, leading them to self-sabotage or be "too conservative" as a result. This rhetoric was further perpetuated in 2013, when Sheryl Sandberg featured the now infamous HP study in her book *Lean In*, which found women would only apply for positions where they could check all 10 out of 10 boxes listing the required skill sets/experiences. We now know that this behavior is influenced by gender biases that have proven women are evaluated on their performance and failure, particularly in male-dominated spaces, which can bring about severe consequences.

But more recent research on how women navigate stressful situations and evaluate risks challenges the widespread notion that women are risk averse. One study, published in 2019 by the Journal of Empirical Finance, set out to understand why companies with female board members made better acquisition and investment decisions alongside less aggressive risk-taking, all while yielding benefits for shareholders. What they discovered was that female board members helped temper the overconfidence of male CEOs and, as a result, made far better strategizing decisions for the long-term health of the company. Researchers noted that "female directors tend to be less conformist and more likely to express their independent views than male directors."[62]

Academic research has proven that financial risk tolerance is not correlated to gender but rather income uncertainty and net wealth.[63] At a broad societal level, it's the aggregation of individual differences in resources and expectations, not anything inherent about gender, that drives risk tolerance. There is, however, an interesting delineation between genders during stressful situations in which heart rates and cortisol levels are heightened. Researchers at Utrecht University found that men make bigger gambles for rewards in stressful situations than they normally would and pay less attention to higher risk losses. Women, on the other hand, pursued smaller wins that were more attainable and had fewer downsides.[64] Furthermore, research out of Wharton found that men's high testosterone levels make them less likely to question their impulses and more prone to thinking they're right even when they are wrong.[65]

Given all this, it would be more accurate to describe women as risk aware, not risk averse. What these research findings showcase is the beauty of balance between masculine and feminine strengths in similar positions of power. Seated around the same table as men, women provide a much needed diversity of thought and perspective to an otherwise homogenous group. Their deviation from the male default when it comes to decision-making isn't a negative, it's a positive. Furthermore, appetite for risk exists on a continuum, not an oversimplified binary of risk taker versus risk averse.

Crossing the Bridge of Calculated Risk

You won't be able to enter the final phase of this journey without taking a risk. The step between testing out options and committing to one is known as crossing the bridge of calculated risk. Picture standing at the entrance to this bridge. At first glance, the bridge might appear treacherous, even a bit shoddy. Your mind starts to race, "Can this actually support my weight? Are those gaps between the wooden planks so big I could fall through them? Is that rope fraying?" You shiver a little but decide to proceed anyway. Then the next test comes when you make the mistake of looking down. You now see the deep ravine beneath the bridge, with jagged rocks all the way at the bottom that look like they could cause irreparable damage if you fell through the gaps. Those jagged rocks represent all of the things that can keep you stuck on this side of the bridge, namely your inner critics, external opinions, and your comfort.

> **Inner Critics.** These are the nasty inner voices that judge and criticize your every effort. They team up with your biases, trying to convince you that change is bad, the risk is far greater than it actually is, and that this move could be catastrophic. It sounds a little silly when you say what your inner critics are saying out loud, but when those voices are yelling at you in your head, their messages can seem so real and convincing.

> **External Opinions.** The fastest way to veer off your chosen path is focusing on what others think you should do versus what you know you need to do. There may be people in your life who mean well and offer you unsolicited (or even solicited) advice. While they believe they're acting in a way that's best for you, they are also offering you guidance from their own view of the world and experiences. Even if others aren't telling you what you "should" be doing, sometimes just the anticipation of what they might

say or think about you can cause us to doubt our choices.

Comfort. It might seem counterintuitive that comfort could present itself as a jagged rock that might destroy us, but it's likely the most jagged of them all. Comfort represents the known. It is the "safe" option you're currently in, which might not be great, but at least you know what you're up against. By stepping onto the bridge of calculated risk, you're inevitably going to face challenges or, even scarier, opportunities you may not have encountered before, and what if you aren't equipped to handle them?

It is normal to reach this point of the journey and have doubts. There is a degree of risk in making this change precisely because there are unknowns that you can't know until you commit to moving forward. But you also know that your current state is unsustainable, which is why you began this entire process in the first place. It's just a matter of time before you will have to deal with leaving your comfort zone, either now or in the future.

The tension between sticking to what we know and honoring who we are becoming was a tension that Burunda Prince became very familiar with throughout her career. After graduating from MIT with a chemical engineering degree, Burunda began working at P&G where her brilliance was quickly recognized. It wasn't long before she was tasked to lead a team of engineers to create an all-in-one shampoo and conditioner product. At the time this had never been done, and Burunda's team would go on to successfully invent what is known today as the Pert Plus 2-in-1.

By all measures, Burunda was thriving in her career. But she had noticed through the experience of designing this new product that the people with true influence were on the business side, not in her department of R&D. She began to explore what it would take to make this transition; she knew she was meant to run a business, despite being a phenomenal engineer.

Burunda applied to several MBA programs and, within a year, she crossed the bridge of calculated risk to Harvard Business School. Over the next two years, she would earn her MBA and launch her career in consulting.

Admittedly, this first bridge didn't seem so risky to Burunda. She had only invested a couple of years into engineering, and now she was armed with a degree from one of the top business schools in the country. Worst case scenario, she could always turn back to engineering as an even more attractive candidate. Little did she know it was the next bridge that would truly test her.

After graduating from Harvard Business School, Burunda began working as a management consultant for Bain & Company. Although she enjoyed the work, a trusted advisor told her she couldn't make partner if she had kids. Thankfully, not all consulting companies were so blatantly toxic and misogynistic, so Burunda moved to Rohm and Haas, where blending her chemical background and business experience gave her a significant advantage. Now she was really coming into her own, and she continued to thrive in her career over the next twelve years.

During that time, Burunda got married and had three beautiful children. But the act of juggling these responsibilities became increasingly difficult. With growing activity schedules, two high-powered careers that required both her and her husband to travel frequently, and no family close by to provide support, things were getting chaotic. Then, one day, Berunda was listening to an NPR interview with Cokie Roberts. "I've learned you can have it all," Roberts said about balancing work and career. "You just can't have it all at the same time." That message touched Burunda deep inside, and she knew it was time to take a step back to assess what truly was important to her.

Both she and her husband felt it was important for them to be the primary caretakers of their children, especially as their kids got older. With her oldest in fifth grade and her youngest in first, the kids were rapidly approaching an age where Burunda wanted to be engaged and involved in their lives. Again, Burunda found herself at a fork in the road, facing a big decision. For the first time since college, her career was no longer her top priority. But what would this mean for her? Would she be throwing away her career? Would she ever want to return to corporate?

As fate would have it, Burunda's company was "rightsizing," a fancy word for layoffs, and Burunda took this as a sign to once again cross the bridge of calculated risk, leaving her corporate job to be at home full-time with the kids. "There are very few things that are written in stone," she told me. "I've learned this over the years, and it's given me a sense of freedom to take the leap. If it doesn't work, I can do something about it. But I am not stuck here."

This decision took Burunda down a path she never could have envisioned while working full-time. Over the next nine years, she ran for public office twice, becoming the board VP of her school district. Channeling her work experience during her tenure in office, she rallied a team that would move their district from the lower quartile to ranking number one out of 700 school districts in the state. All of these opportunities and accomplishments remained invisible and unknown until she honored who she was becoming and took a leap of faith.

Burunda's story is a reminder that we'll never have all of the information we need before committing to a decision. There is no crystal ball that tells us how it all turns out. There is no guarantee that crossing the bridge of calculated risk will end up being a good move—just like there is no guarantee that it will be a bad one. You have to trust that you made the best decision you could with the information you had, and you have to trust that there's always another move you can make.

The best decisions are made with both external data

and internal intuition. Our intuition is incredibly accurate after we've gathered insights and data about our next move, but we can't move forward if we stay stuck in what we know. We can't cross the bridge if we keep staring at the rocks below.

Until now, you've been on a fact-finding mission. You built your foundation by assessing your experiences, uncovering your priorities and values, and understanding what's most important to you in this unique stage of your life and career. Then, through the activation and testing phase, you went on a fact-finding mission to gain data, information, and support, all of which informed your best next step. Now you stand here, at the edge of your bridge, faced with a choice.

Close your eyes, take a deep breath, and tune into your intuition. When it speaks, listen. Choose courage and then run toward who you are becoming.

3

BELIEF
+
COMMITMENT
=
MOMENTUM

Momentum

[mo • men • tum]

1. The force or energy gained by a moving object

2. The quantity of motion of a moving body, measured as a product of its mass and velocity.

This final section is arguably the most important. All of the knowledge you've gained and the work you've done are incredibly valuable, but how you use that information to move forward is where true momentum builds.

Throughout the previous chapters, we've explored the tension between external and internal. In section one, we examined the internal psychology that impacts our behaviors and the external factors that impact our reality. As we moved into section two, we learned that designing a career requires the internal work of building our foundation followed by finding and inviting external support into our lives. In this final section, we'll navigate balancing internal momentum with external movement to move you toward a life and career in alignment with who you are becoming.

Internal Momentum

The act of building an aligned life and career is not a one and done process, although that's tempting to believe. Our tendency to believe we're all set once we've been through this alignment process once is what psychologists call the end of history illusion. We've already discussed this phenomenon at the start of section two, but it's so important it bears repeating. When we reflect on the past, we can recognize that our desires and motivations have changed. But when we consider the future, we assume that we'll remain the same. But remember, that tendency is an illusion; who we are today is not who we will be tomorrow. We continue to change over the course of our life in both small and big ways. Which also means that our careers will naturally evolve as we evolve. In fact, we should expect and normalize this shift. It's common across genders and fields and ages. It's just not part of our cultural narrative yet.

Sara started her career as an aspiring professional opera singer in NYC. She had used the last of her savings to join a program designed to help her develop her personal brand as a singer in the hopes that it would be what she needed to get her big break. Each week of the program, Sara got a different assignment that ranged from establishing her core values, explaining why she wanted to sing, and detailing what she wanted her life to look like, both personally and professionally. Through this experience, Sara realized she had been maniacally pursuing a career that was deeply misaligned with what mattered to her most.

Although she no longer aspired to sing professionally, Sara wanted to stay connected to music. She took a development internship with Carnegie Mellon while she figured out her next move and discovered she loved the work, but she also needed something that offered a livable salary. She began applying for similar roles and eventually moved out to San Diego to work as the Development Associate for Individual Giving at La Jolla Playhouse. She loved the working environment there and quickly discovered that she had a gift for asking people for large sums of money. For the next few years, Sara knew this was where she was meant to be and what she was meant to be doing.

But as time went on, Sara again sensed a growing disconnect between her work and what mattered to her. Despite raising millions for the nonprofit, she was still living largely paycheck to paycheck. She wanted to build for her future, not just have enough money to get by. Sara went back to the exercises she had learned in New York to figure out what her next career move might look like. She had two realizations. The first was that her fundraising work was just a form of sales and sales had the potential to be far more lucrative. The second was that music still wasn't a viable full-time job. She had continued singing in her free time and that was enough to keep her connected to music.

Armed with this knowledge, Sara applied to a local software startup that sold to nonprofits. She was hired as a sales rep and once again found herself aligned and thriving. In her first year, she became a top performer and was promoted to Team Lead. But work was not her driving force anymore—she had started dating someone seriously, and they were talking about getting married, having a family, and settling down. But they didn't see a future in San Diego. Sara was also realizing that while she had loved sales, sales management was not aligned with what she wanted.

Eager to make a change and start their new life together, Sara grew impatient for her next career move. When an opportunity for a remote position selling technology consulting services to nonprofits fell into her lap, Sara accepted before vetting the role to see if it was aligned with what she wanted. Free to work from anywhere, Sara and her husband relocated to her hometown of Durham, NC. Immediately, Sara realized she had made a mistake. She stuck with the job because it afforded her the ability to buy their first home and support her husband, who had just bought a struggling restaurant. Relationships were most important to her in this season of life, so she made a few small adjustments to make the role work for her, like joining a coworking space so she didn't feel so isolated as a remote worker.

Over time, Sara and her husband noticed that the restaurant they owned flourished when both of them were involved. Sara was surprised to find that the more involved she became in the restaurant, the happier she was. By this point in her career, Sara was so proficient at tuning into her intuition that she started making preparations for a transition. Within a year, she left her job in consulting and went full-time as CEO of their hospitality group. Since then, Sara shepherded the company through the global pandemic in 2020 and expanded the business portfolio to include a brewery, a coffee shop, and multiple restaurants in North Carolina.

Sara's career journey was an iterative process. She noticed when her priorities shifted and allowed them to be as fluid as they needed to be, shifting from career to family to career again. Each time Sara crossed the bridge of calculated risk, it was still scary. Each of her decisions still had significant unknowns. But each time she decided to go through the process of realignment, she accumulated experience and learned that she could trust that intuitive voice when it spoke to her. She eventually welcomed it rather than fearing what it would ask of her.

Living in our fullest potential is an ongoing journey, not a destination to be achieved. We create momentum on that journey when we combine the belief that we can and will change over time with a commitment to a growth mindset. Momentum and confidence build each time we go through the process of deepening our self-knowledge and assessing what's most important to us in our current season of life.

External Momentum

Which leads us to the second form of momentum we're cocreating in this new era of work. Whether we realize it or not, our individual decisions to prioritize aligning our careers with what's most important to us has a far-reaching impact. We're creating external momentum; we're normalizing that change, specifically professional change, is a part of growth and a part of life. We're living proof that navigating a career is not a race to the end but a series of bends and turns on the road of finding fulfillment, success, and a sustainable work life. We are creating ripples.

There is also something much bigger at play in our working culture today. It's very likely that the pandemic marked the start of a new era. People are striving to change the way they work—namely, finding alternative ways to work on their own terms. Since 2020, there has been a 57% increase in fractional executives.[66] Between 2019 and 2021, female founded companies rose 28%.[67] And the ongoing battle over return to work policies are signaling fundamental shifts in the workplace that companies have not yet accepted or, in some cases, are actively fighting against to maintain the status quo.

We are writing history in this very moment, shaping what good will look like in this new era of work. There are predictable patterns from previous eras that we're already seeing play out in the business world. At a high level, the first two decades of a changing work culture are fraught with tension as the new era bumps up against the old and outdated ways of work. People cling to what worked in the past until an individual emerges as the new face of the era—they're held up as the new standard of what good looks like and their practices are widely adopted. At least for the next fifty years until the next era of work begins.

The individual who will serve as this era's catalyst, the person who will shape the way we define and engage in work, is likely already in the workforce now. But the new "standard" for this era won't be fully defined for another fifteen to twenty years. Toward the end of our time together, I'll share why I believe that female founders who are currently scaling their startups might just be the catalysts who will shape the future of work and create a new critical mass of what good looks like.

In the meantime, we are all cocreating external momentum toward a more engaged, nuanced, and flexible approach to career—one in which professional change is no longer dreaded and full of shame but widely expected and even celebrated.

TWELVE

The Power of Pause

"Dig the well before you are thirsty."

—Chinese Proverb

Chances are high that you picked up this book because you already acknowledged the voice inside telling you there was more—more to be had in your career, more to be had in your life as a whole. Maybe you prompted that voice, or maybe a forced change slowed you down enough to hear the voice that had been speaking to you all along.

Whatever started you on this journey, I want to take a moment and reflect on how far you've already come—a moment to look back and see what you've already learned by staying open to the possibility of change. Here's what I want you to remember:

- There is no magic roadmap with an "exit now" sign or step-by-step instructions for our careers.
- Changing careers is normal.
- Our lives occur in seasons, and what is most important to us in each season can and will change.
- Making decisions based on what others think is the fastest way to get off your path of alignment.
- There is no right or wrong. There is only the next best decision based on the information you have.

You are now equipped with a framework to navigate the shift you're in and any future career transitions. But how will you know when it's time for a change? How can you recognize that inner voice when it speaks to you again? The answer lies in leveraging the power of pauses.

On the Spot Reflection

The workplace has grown increasingly volatile. Creating career momentum in the current workplace demands reflection and the capacity to recognize when you need to take a step back in order to move forward. Our ability to acknowledge symptoms of discontent and misalignment—even that inner cry for more—only grows in importance the more we experience the modern-day hustle expected from just about everyone.

Too often, the opposite happens. We get busier during times when we need to be still. Pausing is countercultural, so rather than dealing with negative emotions that crop up as the result of our fast-paced lives, we avoid, suppress, or even reject them. We judge ourselves for feeling the way we do and force ourselves to focus on positive things. This is what psychologists refer to as toxic positivity.

Not all positivity in the face of difficult situations is problematic. In fact, research has shown that looking for silver linings in uncontrollable contexts, such as losing your job, can be highly beneficial. But positivity can quickly turn toxic in controllable situations where we could make a change but avoid doing so because it involves acknowledging negative emotions. When we deny or avoid unpleasant emotions, though, they just get bigger. And we lose the valuable information they bring with them.

In her book *Emotional Agility*, Dr. Susan David recommends approaching strong negative emotions with curiosity. Ask yourself, "What the func?" Func being short for function, of course. What is the emotion trying to tell you? What's buried underneath that emotion?

The practice of tuning into strong emotions instead of denying or avoiding them has been a go-to move throughout Aletha Burgess's career. Just a few years into her career, Aletha had a great job at General Electric. She was passionate about her work, surrounded by incredible teammates, and things were going great, but she couldn't shake the sense that something was off. At first, she shrugged away these unpleasant feelings, but her sense of discontent only grew. So, Aletha turned toward these emotions instead, examining what might be at the root of her discontent. In doing so, she realized that her frustration was directly tied to the city she was living in, not her career.

Equipped with this information, Aletha began exploring internal roles at GE that could take her out of Virginia. Unfortunately, there was nothing available that aligned with what she wanted. Although she enjoyed GE, Aletha knew that location was most important. Being closer to friends and family was a priority at this stage of her life and career. She began searching outside the company for work and eventually secured a position at the Home Depot in Atlanta, GA.

For the next couple of years, things were great. Aletha enjoyed reconnecting with her family and friends and work was going well. She was promoted to Associate Implementation and Planning Manager, where she oversaw store resets for 1,800 stores. It was a huge opportunity, but once again Aletha began sensing a growing discontent. As she got more involved in the role, she learned that store resets couldn't happen while the stores were open during the day. She also discovered that answering questions on site and in real-time during these resets proved more cost effective than overseeing them from afar. Unfortunately, this meant that Aletha worked full days in the office only to be on-call at night in case the reset staff had questions.

After doing this for nearly a year, Aletha knew it was unsustainable. Her strengths as an optimizer were actually working against her in this specific role. Recognizing the misalignment, Aletha began exploring options that might better align with her skill set. Aletha shared that she was ready to make a transition with one of her former colleagues, who encouraged her to consider coming to Bank of America where they now worked. They discussed the culture, the team, and the opportunity, all of which appeared to align with Aletha's priorities, needs, and skills.

So began Aletha's fourteen year tenure at Bank of America and her ascension to Senior Vice President for a top ranked Fortune 500 company. During her time there, Aletha continued making adjustments to her career as her priorities shifted, first moving from Atlanta to Charlotte, then starting a family. Each time she needed a shift, Aletha would sense the voice inside speaking to her again. She had learned early in her career that a willingness to pause and inspect that voice was a hallmark of her success. Rather than avoid the discomfort, she tuned in.

If you're sitting there thinking how great this sounds for Aletha but questioning your own capacity to unpack your emotions, that's totally normal. Moving toward discomfort is a skill like any other—it takes time to develop. In the meantime, consider enlisting some outside support.

During one of the interviews I conducted, I asked a female tech founder how she had managed to navigate the highs and lows of building a business during a global pandemic. "I was going to therapy regularly at the time," she told me, "and I noticed that I was always talking about work during my session." When she mentioned this in passing to a friend, the friend suggested that she consider getting an executive coach. The founder smiled at me as she said, "Turns out an executive coach is just a therapist for work."

If you want to know something about yourself, you can't expect to figure it out while you're running one hundred miles an hour and never stop. Enlisting a coach can help you create the necessary space for self-reflection. "It's so disrespectful to yourself to not take the time to sit down, look into your eyes, and ask yourself 'what do you have to say?'" says executive coach Amy K Musson when asked about the importance of pausing. After working with driven professionals for nearly two decades, she continues to find that it's incredibly powerful when people are willing to "sit with what they want."

Whether you decide to work with a coach or not, the key to moving forward is honoring your emotions, not denying or running away from them. It's ok to feel what you feel. Give life to those emotions, especially the negative ones. Approach them with curiosity and mine them for insights. They'll be there, I promise.

Career Health Checks

Pausing to reconnect with ourselves via a career health checkup can be a powerful proactive step in moving our careers forward. The concept of a career health check is not that different from getting an annual physical exam to check your vitals, run some baseline tests, maybe even bring up a question or two about something small you noticed that you're wondering if you should be concerned about. Typically, you walk out of this appointment with a clean bill of health, maybe a recommendation or two, and you're on your way. But sometimes these checkups surface abnormalities that require additional testing. They alert you that there could be a problem in the future even though you don't have any obvious symptoms now. Regardless of the diagnosis, you learn valuable information that informs how you move forward.

Physical health checks are normalized because we know the value of making sure everything is as it should be. We know our physical health impacts the quality of our life. But we don't apply this same logic when we think about the quality of our careers. We don't take the necessary steps to check our career health "just to be safe." Maybe it's time that shifted. As a society, careers have become an increasingly significant part of our lives. According to the Bureau of Labor Statistics, the average full-time female employee works 8.28 hours per day and full-time male employees work 9.05 hours per day. On the surface, this may not seem noteworthy; you might even think these numbers are low. But let's look at them again through a different lens.

If we assume that you sleep eight hours a night (I know...just humor me for the sake of the numbers), then you're awake for 112 hours in a seven day week. Using the US average for women's work hours, you work at least 41.4 hours every seven days, which means that 37% of your waking hours are dedicated to this one dimension of your life. Put another way, we spend over a third of our awake hours working. If we were to evenly distribute our time amongst all six dimensions of our lives, they would each account for 18.6% of our week. Work consumes twice that, even if it is not a current priority dimension.

When looking at our careers this way, it seems reckless not to prioritize a career health check. Whether we like it or not, work is a large part of our lives, and it affects the other five priority dimensions too. Just think about a time when you had a bad boss. That dynamic didn't stay at the workplace; it permeated your quality of life. Imagine if, once a year, you ran a diagnostic to check your work vitals. You intentionally set aside time to slow down for a beat and examine how things are going. In doing so, you might catch early warning signs that there's misalignment somewhere, or perhaps you spot an increasingly toxic environment. You might even catch a positive signal that you desire more in your professional life.

Imagine if there were go "here" and do "this" signs and ads, encouraging us to take our free career health check, recommended twice a year. Our workplaces would be fundamentally different.

The good news is that we can still prioritize a career health check without these external signs. We can intentionally slow down and reflect to ensure the health of our own professional well-being—just like you're doing now.

There are two more proactive pauses we can incorporate into our careers to deepen our understanding of self and tune into our inner voice. We'll look into those next.

THIRTEEN

The Power of QXRs

> "Our deepest fear is not that we are inadequate. Our deepest fear is that we are powerful beyond measure. It is our light, not our darkness, that most frightens us."
>
> —Marianne Williamson

This next proactive pause, called a QXR, was inspired by an exercise I used to do as a sales executive. As part of the executive team, one of my responsibilities was to report on the state of sales in our company every quarter. When the time rolled around, I'd share our historical results, the progress we'd made toward our annual targets, and the plan for our next quarter.

In preparation for this meeting, I ran reports, reviewed progress on our key initiatives and annual targets, tracked how we were progressing toward our annual goals, and noted any lessons learned or things that didn't go as planned. That data was then used to inform the plan moving forward, either building confidence in where we were headed or highlighting a growing disconnect that needed to be addressed. Over the years, I found that whether the numbers were great or not so great, the quarterly review process left me feeling empowered. I knew my business, I knew what was at the root of our issues, and I had a plan to achieve success.

These reviews were so enlightening that I wondered if there were other ways to experience the benefits of this type of exercise outside of a company context. That thought led me to create the Quarterly X-Factor Review, or QXR for short.

The QXR is a quarterly review for the business of YOU. This is not just a moment to review your career in isolation, it's a moment to examine all the dimensions of your life. The X-factor is a variable for you to define based on what's most relevant to you in this season of your career. This quarterly process involves setting aside dedicated time to reflect on what you've learned and accomplished over the past three months and capture key metrics and insights while they're still front of mind. These reviews are incredibly valuable because they take into account a long enough period of time where it's possible to recognize emerging trends but not so long that you'll forget important details.

Doing regular QXRs is beneficial beyond catching alignment issues early. They also have the power to offset the very real headwinds we discussed at the beginning of the book—the ones working against us when we feel the need to pivot in our careers. The QXR helps you stay focused on what matters most, remember that you're multidimensional, foster confidence, and find clarity. Let's go through each of these benefits in more detail so you can start conducting your own QXRs.

Stay Focused on What Matters Most

By consistently reviewing your goals, your learnings, your accomplishments, and your growth, you have the ability to reassess and refine your goals over the coming months. Establishing a consistent, recurring rhythm dedicated to this reflection helps you stay focused on what matters most. Just like a career health checkup, a QXR can help you spot growing misalignments based on where you're spending your time and energy.

Remember You're Multidimensional

I had a client who came to me quite defeated about how her year was wrapping up. She had done an annual review for work and, despite hitting her goals, she was frustrated—she hadn't seen the typical growth she was used to. When I asked her to update her work review to include all dimensions of her life, the bigger picture of her year came into focus. She had decided early on to prioritize her personal and romantic relationships that year. With this more holistic perspective in place, she smiled.

"I suppose it has been an extremely successful year with tremendous growth in those areas." I was glad she could see it, but she wouldn't have been able to had we not considered that X-factor.

The QXR is a recurring reminder that you are a whole person, not just an employee, not just a producer of goods and services. This helps us avoid the enmeshment trap of thinking we're our work or job title, and it encourages us to acknowledge our identities outside of our work. The QXR helps us explore all dimensions of our lives and capture what we, as whole people, have accomplished.

Foster Confidence

Research has found that women's confidence grows over 3X as much as men's confidence between the ages of 25 and 60.[68] The reason for this is rooted in experience; the more experience a woman has, the more confident she becomes. The caveat of this growth is that experience alone isn't sufficient. She also needs to fully claim what she's done and acknowledge her role in the success. The QXR is a space for you to take full credit for how much you've learned and accomplished, and grow your confidence as a result. You move from guesswork at why you've been successful to understanding how you got where you are and how to repeat that success. This knowing, recognition, and clarity fosters confidence as you move forward.

Find Clarity

I had a client who recently left their job as a sales leader. The job had not been what they were expecting when they came onboard, and they got on our call together with a lot of confusion around where to go next. Although not an ideal way to go about it, I asked them to fill out a QXR for the entire previous year so we could get a more complete view. As we began reviewing their learnings and accomplishments, a theme began to emerge. The type of work that had been most satisfying went beyond the typical role of a sales leader. They had gotten to do these things because they were working for an earlier stage company. Without leaders in marketing or customer service, they had taken on more of a go to market position. We then reviewed the skills they gained over the course of the year and where they derived most of their energy. Through this process, it was clear they had outgrown a sales leadership role. Coupling this with their experience prior to the year, they started recognizing that the next phase of their career was becoming CEO of a scaling startup rather than staying limited (and frustrated) in a sales leadership position. Equipped with this knowledge, they set out to learn more about what it would take to become CEO, eventually connecting with a founder at an early stage startup who was looking for a CEO to help them build and scale the company.

As you continue doing these QXRs, your clarity will increase. At the end of the year, you'll be able to look over the headlines of each QXR and more easily conduct a year in review, spot patterns/trends, and see how far you've come. With this valuable information at your fingertips and your deep understanding of self, you'll be better able to determine the best next steps in your journey.

Now that you know what a QXR is, let's talk through the key elements of a QXR: organizing your thoughts via containers, summarizing your insights in a 4-box summary, and, finally, coming up with goals and initiatives.

Organizing Your Thoughts Via Containers

One way of tracking and remembering what happens over the course of a few months is to use containers where you can drop quick notes to yourself throughout the quarter. This "container" can be any medium that works best for you. A Google doc, the Notes app on your phone, a notebook, etc. Drop your wins and learnings into your chosen container in the months between your official QXRs. A few things to keep in mind as you do this:

- Don't be modest or selective. Aim for quantity of these notes over quality. Maybe you got a Slack message from a coworker that meant a lot, or maybe you worked out every day that week. Whatever stands out, drop it into the container.
- Remember, the QXR reviews both work and personal dimensions of your life.
- When possible, be specific and include metrics, comparisons, etc.

- Sometimes learning what doesn't work is just as powerful as figuring out what does. When you notice things that don't work, when you come up short of a goal, etc. drop them in your container.
- Make sure to leave enough information about each note you put in your container so you can remember it fully when it's time for your QXR.

Summarize Your Insights in a 4-Box Summary

This is where you'll summarize all of the rich information you captured in your container and track any key metrics from the previous quarter. Think of the highlight and lowlight boxes as your headlines. You want to include enough information to remember what you're saying but try to keep each bullet to a single sentence.

Highlights	**Metrics**
• Launched a new podcast • Went on a date every week with my spouse • Retained a major client that was ready to cancel	• Avg. Work Travel Time: 50% • Dates with Spouse: 12 • Friend Hang: 0 • Podcast Subscribers: 30
Lowlights	**Goals**
• Work travel rose to an average of 50% • I did not hang out at all 1:1 with any of my friends	• Prioritize spending time in the areas that are most important to me (relationships) • Explore ways to monetize the podcast

Include any metrics you want to keep front of mind and monitor over the course of the year in the Metrics section. Be mindful of what you choose to include in this box—it can change as your priorities and objectives shift throughout the year. What you measure is critical to informing any changes you want to make moving forward, so choose the metrics that serve as true measurements of what matters most to you at this point in your life.

In the final box, you'll write down your goals. Remember, these goals are intended to guide you rather than deterministically take you step-by-step on some GPS route.

This 4-box summary will become the snapshot view of each quarter. You'll refer back to it in the coming months and years. It's also a great launching point for a conversation with a trusted advisor if you want perspective on your career trajectory.

Come Up With Goals + Initiatives

This final section helps you turn your insights into action. Here you'll include any objectives or smaller goals that further your overarching directional goal. If you find yourself stuck, consider getting outside help. Can you strategize with your boss? Is this hangup something you could work through with a coach? Would a mentor be able to help? Maybe there's a podcast, article, or book you could use as a resource. Remember, the key thing is simply coming up with a few steps to get you started toward your goal. You can always update the plan as you acquire additional information, insights, and clarity.

It's also vital to remember that this section is a "Should Free Zone." A common mistake I see people make the first time they do this part of the QXR is throwing out a few aspirational self goals. It can be easy to fall into old patterns, so keep an eye out for phrases like "I should ______" or "I need to be better at ____________." Those phrases signal internal conflict. If you see them cropping up, take a moment to inspect what's driving them.

As you start integrating QXRs into your routine, here are a few things to keep in mind:

The first time is the hardest. The first time you do your QXR, it may seem like a lot. And it probably is because you're developing a new habit. Much of what you'll be doing for your first QXR is foundational work that you can build off of in the future. Remember, this time is an investment in you and living to your fullest potential. The initial lift is worth it because your satisfaction is worth it.

Regularly document insights. Reviewing several months at a time can be a challenging task to complete "on-demand." Ideally, you'll be capturing notes, insights, praise from your coworkers, etc. in your container as the weeks progress. That way, when you work on your QXR, you simply need to look at your treasure trove of notes and add to it rather than trying to remember things at the end of every three-month period.

Accomplishments come in all shapes and sizes. Dictionary.com defines "accomplishment" as something that has been achieved, carried out, or finished. When it comes to documenting accomplishments for your QXR, focus on quantity over quality. It's far easier to take something out later than trying to remember something you didn't write down because it felt too inconsequential.

Block out time for the QXR process. It's crucial to be intentional about when and how you sit down to do your QXR. Consider blocking out multiple times on your calendar to allow ample time to process your insights and come back to your draft with a fresh set of eyes in case you overlooked something. During that blocked time, give yourself the things you need to mentally be at your best. For some, that might mean scheduling time afterward with a trusted friend, mentor, or coach to keep yourself accountable to investing time in yourself. For others, that might mean celebrating the work you did over the past quarter. Whatever it is, give yourself permission. You deserve the time and energy it takes to be at your best in every dimension of life.

FOURTEEN

Career Sabbaticals

> "Having more control over your time and options is becoming one of the most valuable currencies in the world."
>
> —Morgan Housel

There may come a time in your career when the best path forward is to opt out for a bit. I know, opting out goes against everything you've been told. You might even be thinking of skipping this chapter because the idea seems so out of reach. But stick with me.

You've probably got some version of this advice, which has been blindly handed down from generation to generation: "the best time to find a job is when you have a job." I vividly remember getting this advice from both my parents and my boomer mentor early in my career when I considered leaving my job at a property management company. These were people I trusted, and their strongly worded advice solidified the belief that I should never leave a job without another lined up. It also made me inherently suspicious of people who did have breaks in their resume. Then I experienced a forced change in my career in which I found myself without a job for an extended period of time. That experience woke me up to the fact that I wasn't alone—62% of Americans have taken a career break.[69] Eventually, I shed the belief that had been handed down to me; I now see changes and breaks in our careers as normal, even expected.

Career breaks and sabbaticals have been on the rise since the global pandemic in 2020. The number of millennials who took a career sabbatical nearly doubled in the four years following the pandemic.[70] In my research, I found that one out of four female professionals took career sabbaticals with the intention of stepping back so they could figure out their best next step. This widespread change has prompted professional networking platforms like LinkedIn to launch new features so that professionals can now designate a period of time in their working history as a "Career Break" and include a brief description.

There are many factors that can lead to a career break being the best next step forward, including family responsibilities, caring for a newborn, personal health issues, pursuing education, unsustainable work conditions—the list is endless. What prompts a career break and what that break looks like is as varied as those who experience it.

Specifically for this chapter, we're going to focus on what a career sabbatical might entail so that the option of taking one seems less scary.

Let's start with the basics. Much like an academic sabbatical, a career sabbatical is an extended period of time away from work. According to Harvard Business Review, there are three types of career sabbaticals: working holidays, free dives, and quests.[71]

1. **Working Holidays.** These are often taken by employees who feel pulled to work on another project but don't have the time to pursue it while shouldering their usual responsibilities. During their time away, they alternate between intense periods of work on their chosen project and intentional periods of rest. Often, after ending this kind of sabbatical, employees return to their previous jobs.
2. **Free Dives.** In this type of sabbatical, individuals follow their wanderlust to travel. Often, these sabbaticals include intense periods of exploration which then require rest and time to recharge. Individuals typically set aside time to evaluate their lives prior to their sabbatical, assessing what brought them fulfillment and what made them feel disconnected or unhappy. When these sabbaticals end, people usually return to the same profession they were in prior but pick a job that's better aligned with their values.

3. **Quests.** This type of sabbatical is one in which individuals feel pushed out of work due to an unsustainable work environment. Maybe it's a toxic culture or demands that are causing burnout, but whatever the case, individuals feel that a sabbatical is the only option because they can't stand the environment any longer. Typically, these sabbaticals start with a heavy rest phase so individuals have the chance to recharge and heal. Often, people do not return to their former profession after their sabbatical ends, picking radically new directions for their careers instead.

Consistent across all types of sabbaticals is taking time to reflect on our lives, deepen our understanding of ourselves and our needs, and move forward with intention once that break comes to an end.

Career Sabbatical Landmines

There are some common landmines that can trip you up as you consider or prepare for a career sabbatical. These landmines are very effective at making you second-guess your decision while on leave, especially if this is your first break. Some of these hazards are self-inflicted while others come from people in your network who are unfamiliar with sabbaticals or still deeply entrenched in the old ways of viewing career breaks. Regardless, it's helpful to know what they are so you can prepare for them before stepping on one unaware.

4. **Break = No Work.** A common misconception with career sabbaticals is that you won't be doing work because you're not working in a traditional job. While rest is an important part of a sabbatical, there is also a tremendous amount of internal work and personal development that takes place as well. Go into your sabbatical with this mindset; no, you won't be working in the traditional sense, but you will be doing work. If you are a parent, consider keeping your family on the same routine. If your kids go to daycare or after school programs, keep them in those programs during your sabbatical so you can prioritize rest and self-reflection. That isn't to say you can't pick them up early or break the routine every now and then. But it's important to set the precedent with your family and friends that this sabbatical is now your full-time job. You won't be working constantly. In fact, you may often feel like you "should" be doing more. Remember, though, that this type of work requires significant mental and emotional energy, which means you will need more recovery time than you anticipate. You will also be tapping into your creativity, which also requires rest.
5. **"What do you do?"** Trigger Alert! The first time you get asked "What do you do?" while you're on sabbatical will likely send you into a spiral. For many of us, our identity is so tightly tied to our job

title that we feel lost without it. My recommendation is to anticipate hearing this question—because you will—and decide what you want to say beforehand. Have a description ready that conveys the important work you're doing to rediscover yourself. This will reduce the anxiety you feel when you're asked "What do you do?" and it will also normalize taking a career sabbatical.

6. **"You're being lazy."** Those first few days without work will be great. But within the first week, a little panic will set in too. You'll hear a voice in your head telling you a lot of believable nonsense: "you're lazy," "you are losing your drive," "you won't ever work again," etc. etc. It's important to deal with this inner critic by reminding that sucker that taking time away from work doesn't change who you are at your core. It's also important to remember that this is probably the first time in fifteen years that you haven't had a job. Taking a couple weeks just to decompress seems reasonable.
7. **Deleting Your Experience.** As you start to consider reentering the workforce, it's easy to, metaphorically, "hit delete on your experience." Somehow being out of the "grind" for a while brings with it the lie that none of your professional experience prior to this point in your life is relevant. I know this sounds ludicrous, but it can happen...and it's a total lie. If you start to feel this way, focus some

of your time on sabbatical to capture all you've accomplished leading up to this moment, including the expertise and skills you've gained. Consider tapping your network as well to help you remember the value of what's come before.

8. **Shame Spiraling.** You'll likely feel some amount of shame when discussing your sabbatical. That's normal because of the prevailing work culture and the lingering beliefs handed down from previous generations. The grind and the hustle are still glorified. It's easy to feel like an outsider when you're on sabbatical because it feels like you're doing something no one else dares to do, therefore it must be wrong. Let's reframe this. Sure, some people might view slowing down as the wrong move. But if you've figured out a way to live without working nonstop, doesn't that make you lightyears ahead?
9. **"How nice you'll get to spend more time with your family."** If you're a mother, chances are high that you'll hear this comment more than once. Society assumes that the only reason you're taking time off of work is to be home with your children. People might even expect it of you. But men rarely hear this same comment, which should clue you in to the disparity of expectation for men versus women. Remember, a sabbatical is about you. If you choose to spend more time with your kids because

that's what you want, then great. But don't do it just because you think it's what you should do since you aren't working. This time is about you, not what others think you should be doing.

10. **Feeling Guilty for Being Able To Afford a Sabbatical.** Being able to take time off work without worrying about money is indeed a privilege, but that doesn't mean you need to feel guilty about it. Let that shit go. You've worked hard to manage your money and make the necessary financial decisions that have allotted you this freedom. Other people's comments, like "must be nice" or "you're so lucky," are less a reflection of you and more about them. Ground yourself in the facts that drove this decision.

Knowing the Numbers

Before jumping into a career sabbatical, you'll need to do some prep work. The first thing to figure out is how much money you need to set aside. Now, I'm by no means a financial advisor, so view the following list as recommendations more than hard and fast rules.

Here are some things to consider before getting started:

- Will your employer pay for your full sabbatical? More companies are offering this as a retention tool, so be sure to check your benefits to see if this option is available at your company.
- What is your weekly spend you need to cover for

the length of your sabbatical?

- How long is your sabbatical? (We'll discuss recommendations for timelines in the next section.)
- If you are beginning a sabbatical due to termination, how long can you live off of your severance package?
- If you don't have severance, what is your financial run rate before you have to have regular income?
- Will you have health insurance coverage?

How do you figure out how much money to set aside for your career sabbatical? Below is a simple equation to get you going:

Weekly Spend X Length of Sabbatical = $ To Save

The amount of time you want to budget for a sabbatical will vary by person, but a helpful target is around three months—enough time to decompress and do some self-discovery before figuring out your next move.

If you were recently fired or laid off and considering using this termination as a catalyst for taking a career sabbatical, there are a few additional things to consider when budgeting. Hopefully you were able to get severance as part of your termination that can serve as a small bridge. You can use the following equation to factor in severance pay:

Severance / % of Weekly Spend Your Salary Contributed Toward = # of Weeks for Sabbatical

You can take more time than the severance covers if your financial situation allows.

Mapping Your Timeline

You'll want to map out a rough timeline for your sabbatical to include a few important milestones:

1. **Time to Decompress.** I suggest setting aside at least a third of your total sabbatical to decompress. You can cut the time down if you feel mentally and emotionally ready for the next stage.
2. **Begin Job Search.** I recommend working backward into this stage based on the average time it takes to go through the interview process. Use conservative estimates when determining this, as it isn't something you have control over. The numbers vary significantly on what's considered average. Recent reports show that the interview process can take anywhere from six weeks to six months. Impacting this number will be the level of position you're applying for, whether you're able to leverage referrals, and whether or not you're changing careers.
3. **Secure Your Next Step.** This is something you've already figured out based on your financial situation. Whether you will be starting your own company or accepting an offer letter, have a goal date to begin your next chapter.

The narrative that the best time to find a job is when you have a job is nothing more than fear mongering over something largely outside our control. Yes, there are still hiring managers out there holding on to this outdated belief, and some 64% of people still believe there's stigma around career breaks.[72] But considering that 84% of individuals who took a career break found it beneficial, I encourage you to stay open to a career sabbatical; stepping back from your current role might be what you need to take that next step forward in your career.

Money expert Morgan Housel wrote this in his bestseller *The Psychology of Money*:

> If you have flexibility, you can wait for good opportunities. You'll feel less urgency to chase and more leeway to find your passion and your niche at your own pace. The ability to do those things when most others can't is one of the few things that will set you apart in a world where intelligence is no longer a sustainable advantage.

We know the system is broken. We know the game is still rigged, especially for women. Rather than change the game, we can change the rules. In the next chapter, we'll discuss why now is an opportune time to disrupt and reimagine a new normal of work.

FIFTEEN

Signals of Change

"History cannot give us a program for the future, but it can give us a fuller understanding of ourselves, and of our common humanity, so that we can better face the future."

—Robert Penn Warren

The year 2020 marked the start of a new era of work. We can see the same seismic shifts taking place in the working world now as we can when looking back at the start of the Information Era—which we have just exited—and the Industrial Era before that. In each of these shifts, there are distinct, almost predictable patterns that mark the important milestones in an era.

Here's how these patterns generally play out: The start of a new era is riddled with angst and turmoil. Changes are beginning to emerge, but rather than recognize the dawn of a new era, leaders cling to the past, using old and outdated practices that no longer work. Within the first ten to fifteen years of the new era, a leader(s) enters the workforce who will fundamentally reshape the working landscape. Somewhere around the twenty to twenty-five year mark, this leader becomes the new standard for "good," establishing the new normal for the next forty-five years until that era ends and another one begins, starting these patterns once again.

To see this play out more fully, let's take a little trip down history lane to the start of the US Industrial Era.

Industrial Era (1870s - 1940s)

The Industrial Era marked a shift from agrarian work and handicraft to industry and machine manufacturing as the primary economic drivers. Rural workers began moving away from family farms and into cities to work at factories.

In the 1870s, a machinist and laborer named Frederick Taylor began to notice that his fellow laborers and their machines were not running as efficiently as they could. When Taylor got promoted to foreman, he set out to fix the high labor costs being driven by this inefficiency. In the 1880s, he created what is now known as Taylorism, which produced two noteworthy principles that radically changed the way companies operated and still shape our modern-day perception of productivity.

The first was applying the concept of averages and

standardization to factories and factory workers. The work environment in which Taylor served as an apprentice was human driven. Companies hired those they deemed most talented, regardless of their skill set, and allowed them to drive design decisions. But Taylor was adamant that businesses should not conform to individuals and their ideas of what processes worked best in the workplace. He believed companies should hire employees who would fit the already-established systems instead. In the long run, he thought, even mediocre employees who followed the plan laid out by management, operating procedures, and policies would prove more successful to a business than any brilliant minds led by inspiration.

Taylor meticulously measured every task within a factory, looking for ways to optimize them. Once he optimized a task, he then measured for the average of how long it took to complete that task. This average then became the standard every employee had to aim for. Taylor repeated this process over and over across the whole factory until he had standardized the entire industrial process. Taylor believed there was a singular best way to accomplish any process; once he determined that process, it became the standard—the one and only way to do that task.

Today, we can still see the effects of this approach play out in the workplace. It resembles those corporate playbooks so prevalent at more established organizations. Employees are given specific instructions for how to successfully execute their jobs, and they're reprimanded whenever they deviate from those instructions or don't uphold specific operating procedures. It seems a bit ironic that the system that allowed Taylor to make his mark on a process and identify the way to improve it would make that same approach nearly impossible for another laborer. Under his own system, Taylor likely would have been told to keep his ideas to himself and just follow the established process.

The second noteworthy shift during the Industrial Era was the concept of management being the executive decision-makers. While this seems obvious today, the concept was radical at the time. Prior to the twentieth century, companies viewed employees who were nonproductive, i.e. sitting at desks rather than doing physical labor on the factory floors, as unnecessary expenses. Why would they hire someone to oversee a job that the person couldn't do themselves? But Taylor argued separating doers from thinkers was a critical step toward driving maximum efficiency. He is quoted as saying, "In our scheme, we do not ask for the initiative of our men. We do not want any initiative. All we want of them is to obey the orders we give them, do what we say, and do it quick."

Over the next thirty years, Taylor standardized every function within the factory system. In 1911, Taylor published *The Principles of Scientific Management* outlining his work. The book quickly became a bestseller, and his principles became known as Taylorism, which became the foundation of today's lean Six Sigma methodology. On the heels of his book's success, Taylor launched the first management consultant business and became a highly sought advisor to manufacturing companies. Even a century later, the Fellows of the Academy of Management voted Taylor's book the most influential management book of the twentieth century, thus continuing—and reinforcing—its impact.

If you've worked for any established company, you have likely experienced the ripple effect of Taylorism. Despite shifting from factory work to the information age, the principles of scientific management persevere. The restrictive belief that once a process is optimized it becomes the only way to do that process is ever-present in company playbooks, where companies continue to abide by standard operating procedures rather than reinvent any part of the wheel or take a chance on hiring someone who doesn't perfectly fit a role. Taylorism perpetuates the belief that there is a singular best way to run a business and execute a task, and a singular best background that someone must have in order to perform well in a position. If you've ever proposed an alternative way to do something or attempted to deviate from the "script" and been told to get back in line and follow the process, then you have experienced the effects of Taylorism.

Much like how Taylorism emerged at the start of the Industrial Era and shaped management best practices moving forward, another man would rise to power at the start of the Information Age and make an equally significant mark on the professional world, shaping the definition of what "good" meant in the workplace for an entire generation of workers.

The Information Age (1950s - 2020)

The shift from the Industrial Age to the Information Age is believed to have occurred in the mid twentieth century. The business climate at the time was rapidly shifting from traditional industries to one driven by information technology. Job opportunities transitioned from primarily manual labor jobs in manufacturing and construction to knowledge-based, office-oriented roles. These new roles relied heavily on information processing and technology skills, often requiring higher education and analytical abilities in order to be successful in them. Earlier in the book, we discussed how this change created clerical work that would lead to women entering the workforce. With new technology, US-based companies were now competing in a global market.

In 1960, a man we've also discussed before, Jack Welch, joined General Electric as a worker in a plastics plant. He was promoted to manager in his first three years and tasked with developing a new plastic. Impatient for results, Welch pushed his team to move faster and increase experiments which jeopardized the safety standards in place at the factory. But this approach backfired, quite literally, when there was a factory explosion. Instead of being fired for his negligence, however, Welch convinced executives to spend $10 million dollars on a new factory to produce a new plastic called Noryl. This product became a billion dollar business, and Welch was promoted to the Head of Plastics Division in 1968. Over the next three years, his division was responsible for doubling sales and inventing several new products.

By 1977, the GE CEO Reginald Jones was winding down his career and preparing to retire. He began creating a short list of executives who could be his successor, and Jack Welch was at the top of the list. Jones wanted to test Welch's abilities, so he gave him a portfolio of businesses to run, including appliances and credit operations. There, Jack deployed what would become his go-to move to boost profits: layoffs.

Cementing himself as an unconventional leader but one that got results no matter the costs, Welch was named CEO of GE in 1981. Welch became what is considered the first celebrity CEO, hanging out with professional athletes and movie stars. During his reign, GE rose to number five on the Fortune 500 list, wielding tremendous influence over both government policies and other executives. GE's Management Development Institute in Crotonville, NY, was nicknamed GE University—the gold standard for management pedigree.

Those in power were willing to overlook both the creative accounting that enabled Welch to consistently exceed quarterly projections and the aggressive tactics that were slowly rotting GE from the inside out. In 1999, Fortune magazine named Welch "Manager of the Century,"and his proteges were heavily recruited to struggling Fortune 500 companies in hopes that they, too, could sprinkle the Welch magic: increased profits (and, of course, increased layoffs). At one point in the early 2000s, nearly 20% of the top thirty companies in Dow Jones Industrial Average were run by men who, at one time, had worked for Welch.

Ironically, and much like Taylor, Welch destroyed the system that allowed him to rise in power. Welch spent his entire forty year career at GE, starting as a factory worker and benefitting from the resources and development programs that gave him opportunities to grow his career within GE. Programs that would later disappear.

Even as tech companies like Microsoft and Google supplanted GE as the new sheriffs in town, Welch's strategies and prioritization of shareholders continued to be the dominant practice.

Age of Automation? Sustainability? Balance? AI? (2020 -)

The global pandemic in 2020 brought with it the start of a new era. The current business practices are no longer working for anyone. Burnout is on the rise for both men and women. More accessible four-year degrees have neutralized their effect; it's no longer a guarantee that pursuing higher education will be a return on investment. Americans are waking up to the reality that more is not better. Despite AI technology existing for nearly fifty years, it is now at the forefront changing the way we work and creating new positions while potentially eliminating others to meet the needs of this new technology.

What does this mean for us? It means that we can become writers of history. Each of us is playing a role in shaping what will become this new era of work, which means we get an opportunity to decide what is written. We can choose to maintain the shame of transitioning careers handed down to us from men like Welch, who experienced all the benefits of career development within a system he then disposed of, or we can choose to normalize the process of change. We can continue tuning into our intuition, giving credence to that voice telling us there's more.

I believe we have a tremendous opportunity to put humans at the center of business again. An opportunity to take a long-term view while still honoring short-term needs. An opportunity to create gender balance in positions of power. It's very likely that the future "face" of this era is already in the workforce or about to enter it. Over the next twenty years, they will make their presence known and usher in the new standard of good. And I believe the "face" to help us get there are female founders building and scaling companies. Let's take a closer look at why.

History Is Repeating

Industrial Era (1880-1950s)

Shift from rural to city for employment opportunity

1880s: Frederick Taylor developed Taylorism

1911: Taylor published his book The Principles of Scientific Management and becomes first "management consultant"

Information Age (1950s - 2020)

Shift from factory to information technology as economic driver

1964: Jack Welch is hired at GE

1981: Jack Welch is made CEO of GE

2000: Jack Welch is named Manager of the Century

New Era (2020 - ?)

We are in the early days of transformation.

The future isn't female. It's balanced.

The rate of female advancement within traditional corporations is painfully slow. Arguably, three generations of women have had full careers since the start of women entering the workplace, and still women are the minority in executive rooms. Even if women do manage to make it to the top, many have had to dim their feminine strengths to get there.

Imagine if, instead of waiting for understanding of our unique strengths and authenticity, instead of waiting for equality in positions of power, we started at the top and set a new standard. Women could build out balanced, diverse, equitable organizations rather than trying to fix one that's broken.

During the fallout from the COVID-19 pandemic, there were early signs that women were losing ground in climbing the ladder. In 2022, women at or above director levels were stepping away from work at unprecedented rates, leaving the media to paint a doomsday message that this great resignation would set women's progress back decades. Simultaneously, however, another trend emerged that received far less attention. The World Economic Forum reported that between 2019 to 2021, there was a 68% increase in female founded companies, and between 2021 to 2023,[73] women made up 47% or more of newly founded companies.[74] Were women really stepping away from their careers or were they leaving broken corporations to build their own companies?

In a strange way, the pandemic might've been the best thing to happen for professional women, opening new opportunities, new paths to pursue, and possibly transforming the world of work in the process.

Women Build Differently

Women build differently than their male counterparts in three key ways: what they build, how they build, and why they build.

What they build. Women build companies to solve problems impacting a community they care about. Often, but not always, these are communities in which there are limited solutions to the problem. Women see problems worth solving that may have been overlooked as inconsequential in the past by those in traditional positions of power or influence. Female founders share a desire to build companies that create a better future for those who are coming behind them so that they don't have to face or solve the same problems that inspired these new companies.

Why they build. In my interviews for this book, I would ask women if entrepreneurship was something they considered for themselves. Their reactions were mixed. Some had known entrepreneurship was for them early on because of their exposure to this world while others felt they had fallen backward into founding a company. Despite what led them to starting a company, they all used the same language to describe why they were building. It was a deep knowing. Each one felt a strong responsibility, an intuitive nudge, or a sense that they were meant to address the situation their company aimed to solve. They recognized their unique ability to see the challenge, and they had the skills, experience, and/or capabilities to address it.

How they build. In his book *The Infinite Game*, Simon Sinek discusses game theory in the business world. There are two types of games: finite and infinite. Finite games are defined by rules, players, and timelines. There are winners and losers. Athletic competitions are examples of a finite game. Infinite games are more ambiguous in nature. The goal is not to win but to stay in the game as long as possible. Players can come and go, and the rules can change at any time. Business is just one example of an infinite game.

We are living with the consequences of leaders like Jack Welch using finite strategies in an infinite game. When women build, they are not fixated on short-term objectives with little or no regard for long-term implications. Rather, they build playing an infinite game, balancing the long-term view with near-term decisions. Their goal is sustainability; they are looking to stay in the infinite game as long as possible to ensure that they can continue addressing the problem they are aiming to solve.

	Women	Men
WHAT THEY BUILD	Companies that solve problems impacting a community where there are limited solutions.	Companies that address a known issue and could make them the next unicorn.
WHY THEY BUILD	Called to build. A knowing that they see a way create a better future for those who come behind them.	Opportunistic. This company could secure their financial freedom and future.
HOW THEY BUILD	Play an infinite game. They prioritize sustainability to ensure they can continue addressing the problem they aim to solve.	Prioritize strategies that accelerate scale and drive hypergrowth.

Another Broken Ladder?

There is tremendous value in women building companies that scale, but the startup space is not immune to biases and headwinds against women. The way startups are coached toward success is built off of a primarily male viewpoint. There is an illusion that the best practices established by successful founders (all of them men) make these practices the only way to succeed—not just one possible way to succeed. Only 20% of these renowned startup unicorns—companies that receive a billion-dollar valuation—had a woman on their senior leadership team.

Not only has the startup ecosystem been built for and by men, but how women build conflicts with the norm of seeing a quick return. There is a high premium placed on accelerated growth and reaching unicorn status. Companies that take funding have a vested interest in rapid growth in order to shorten the timeline for paying back investors.

The singular view of what a "good" startup founder looks and acts like is highly visible and ever present in the funding gap. Of venture capital decision-makers, 88% are men;[75] in 2022, female founders received a horrific 1.9% of venture capital invested.[76] These numbers are even worse for women of color, who received just 0.8% of funding.[77] Although these numbers are bleak, raising capital is not the only path to building a business. Bootstrapping, another term for building without raising capital from investors, is another viable option, especially with 31% of women in heterosexual relationships outearning their partners.[78]

There are tangible benefits to the way women build companies. When women receive funding, they drive two times more revenue per dollar invested compared to men. There is also a proven advantage to having work experience prior to launching a company. Older entrepreneurs have a substantially higher success rate than younger founders. In fact, the average age of a founder looking to scale their company is forty-five.[79] Evidence points to entrepreneurial performance rising rapidly with age before plateauing in the late fifties. And founders with three or more years of prior work experience in the same industry niche as their startup were 85% more likely to launch a highly successful startup.[80]

The future is not female, it is balanced. As more and more women hold positions of power, we will reap the benefits of our diversity of thought and perspectives. But we can only see that benefit when there is mutual respect between men and women for the unique strengths we bring to the work environment. In order for us to realize that future, each of us must take steps toward the areas, industries, and problems where we want to make an impact. That doesn't mean we all have to climb the corporate ladder or scale a startup; it means we have to courageously claim our best next step—whatever it is, however much it varies from the norm—and then take it.

We don't need everyone to want the same thing. We need to do our own work and create our own ripple. Only then can we create waves of change.

SIXTEEN

Creating Ripples

"Once a small win has been accomplished, forces are set in motion that favor another small win."

—Karl Weick

In the late nineteenth century in Pittsburgh, PA, Elizabeth Cochrane was furious after reading an article in her local paper titled "What Girls Are Good For." The article emphasized that a woman's primary purpose was birthing children and maintaining a home. Unwilling to sit back in silence, Cochrane sent a response under the pseudonym Lonely Orphan Girl challenging the article. Her strongly worded response caught the attention of the editor, and he put out an announcement asking the Lonely Orphan Girl to identify herself. When Cochrane came forward as the author, the editor did not reprimand her as Cochrane expected. Instead, he offered her a job.

Cochrane began working under the pen name Nellie Bly, writing a series of investigative articles on women working in factories. After several years and many successful stories, she moved to a bigger market in New York. There, Bly took an undercover assignment investigating mental health facilities. At the time, these facilities were overcrowded and used questionable practices that left patients languishing rather than improving. Bly faked being insane in order to get admitted to one of these facilities and witness firsthand the now infamous Blackwell's Island Asylum. Bly spent ten days in the institution and experienced abhorrent conditions before being released. Using the information she gathered, Bly published her exposé *Ten Days in a Mad-House* that revealed the inhumane practices occurring at the mental health institution. Her actions were a catalyst for a much needed reform of mental health institutions and created an entire field of investigative journalism that continues to exist today.

Her career in journalism began because she acted on an idea, an outrage, and didn't stay silent. She responded to an article at a time when women weren't considered writers. That single decision set into motion a series of events that led to societal change.

Just like Cochrane, your individual actions have a ripple effect. No matter the scale of your ambition or impact, the work you are doing to deepen your self-knowledge, the work you're doing to determine where you want to use your skills—this work is a powerful force for good, even if you can't see the end from where you're standing now. Much like how small winds create ripples, and ripples create powerful waves, your choice to honor that voice inside you is a small win for society. Each time you invest energy into understanding who you are and where you can blend your talents, experiences, and passion with a career, you are building momentum that others will feel and be lifted by. You are changing the direction of society, one courageous choice at a time.

Small Wins Beget Big Shifts

This concept of small wins begetting bigger wins and creating social changes may seem overwhelming or out of reach, but you're already doing it. You've already narrowed your focus to something within your control, something small. That next step is all you need to take to make an impact—that movement alone will build, creating momentum inside and out. Knowing this releases us from the feeling of powerless overwhelm and into a state of action.

Throughout this book, you've learned a series of skills and habits that you can take forward and build upon. The work you've done to establish your personal foundation leads directly into the next phase of inviting others into your journey. You are attracting allies and gathering a solid career crew around you because you can clearly articulate who you are and what you are seeking. Because of your clarity, this trajectory will continue; you'll attract more allies and deter those who don't align with your newfound direction.

I want you to remember that the wide range of experiences you uncovered earlier in this book are a tremendous asset, not something to be ashamed of. They allow you to see parallels between the various dimensions of your life, and they highlight the growth mindset that undoubtedly started you down this path of reassessing your career. Your diverse experiences, hobbies, and interests are rich sets of information that you can pull from as you navigate new territory.

It isn't easy to give up your old sense of self, your old career title, or that dream you thought you were going to pursue your whole life. But it is worth it, and you're not alone in this process of rebecoming.

You no longer have to define yourself by your past experiences; you now have a host of skills, a frame of reference, and a language to speak about yourself in a more fluid way. You've connected the dots of your life and career and can now share that beautiful narrative with others. Chances are high that they'll find aspects of their journey in yours, since the only constant across all of our lives is change. And now you have a way to embrace change—small and big, inside and out—and help others do the same.

I'll leave you with this final question. With understanding of the past and eyes wide open to the challenges ahead, will you choose courage? Courage to honor the voice inside you ready for more? Courage to start your new journey?

Courage to create a ripple that becomes a wave of good? Courage to acknowledge how powerful you truly are?

I hope you continue choosing courage, and I believe you will. Because you've chosen courage to be right where you are, right here, right now.

APPENDIX

LIFELINE EXERCISE

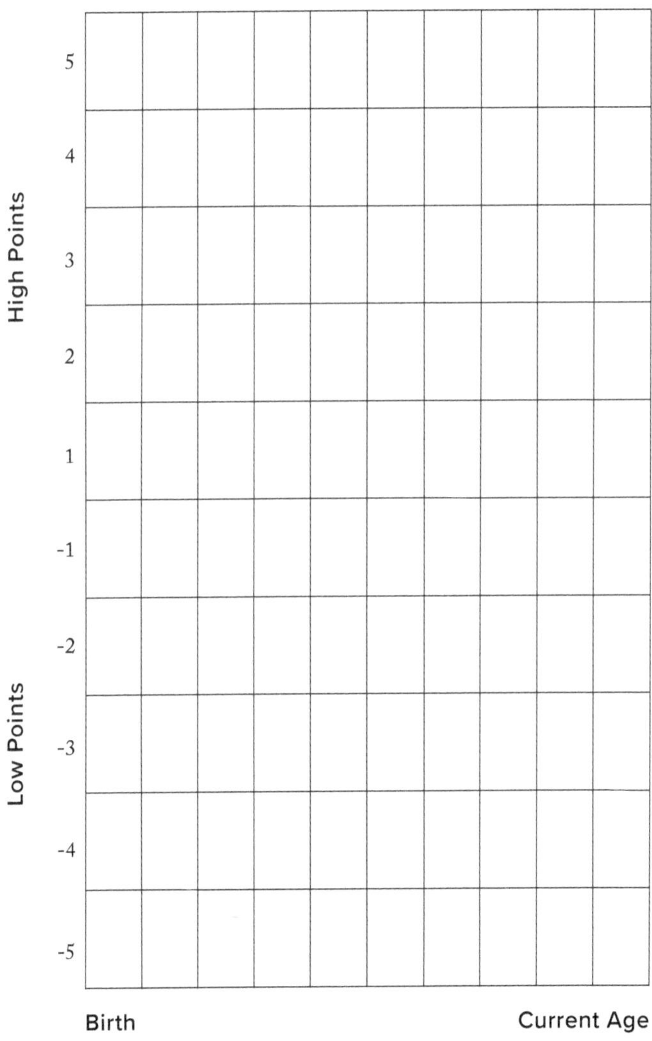

APPENDIX

Core Value Sample Definitions

Acceptance: to be open to and accepting of myself, others, life etc

Adventure: to be adventurous; to actively seek, create, or explore novel or stimulating experiences

Assertiveness: to respectfully stand up for my rights and request what I want

Authenticity: to be authentic, genuine, real; to be true to myself

Beauty: to appreciate, create, nurture or cultivate beauty in myself, others, the environment etc

Caring: to be caring towards myself, others, the environment etc

Challenge: to keep challenging myself to grow, learn, improve

Compassion: to act with kindness towards those who are suffering

Connection: to engage fully in whatever I am doing, and be fully present with others

Contribution: to contribute, help, assist, or make a positive difference to myself or others

Conformity: to be respectful and obedient of rules and obligations

Cooperation: to be cooperative and collaborative with others

Courage: to be courageous or brave; to persist in the face of fear, threat, or difficulty

Creativity: to be creative or innovative

Curiosity: to be curious, open-minded and interested; to explore and discover

Encouragement: to encourage and reward behaviour that I value in myself or others

Equality: to treat others as equal to myself, and vice-versa

Excitement: to seek, create and engage in activities that are exciting, stimulating or thrilling

Fairness: to be fair to myself or others

Fitness: to maintain or improve my fitness; to look after my physical and mental health and wellbeing

Freedom: to live freely; to choose how I live and behave, or help others do likewise

Friendliness: to be friendly, companionable, or agreeable towards others

Forgiveness: to be forgiving towards myself or others

Fun: to be fun-loving; to seek, create, and engage in fun-filled activities

Generosity: to be generous, sharing and giving, to myself or others

Gratitude: to be grateful for and appreciative of the positive aspects of myself, others and life

Honesty: to be honest, truthful, and sincere with myself and others

Humour: to see and appreciate the humorous side of life

Humility: to be humble or modest; to let my achievements speak for themselves

Industry: to be industrious, hard-working, dedicated

Independence: to be self-supportive, and choose my own way of doing things

Intimacy: to open up, reveal, and share myself -- emotionally or physically – in my close personal relationships

Justice: to uphold justice and fairness

Kindness: to be kind, compassionate, considerate, nurturing or caring towards myself or others

Love: to act lovingly or affectionately towards myself or others

Mindfulness: to be conscious of, open to, and curious about my here-and-now experience

Order: to be orderly and organized
Open-mindedness: to think things through, see things from other's points of view, and weigh evidence fairly.
Patience: to wait calmly for what I want
Persistence: to continue resolutely, despite problems or difficulties.
Pleasure: to create and give pleasure to myself or others
Power: to strongly influence or wield authority over others, e.g. taking charge, leading, organizing
Reciprocity: to build relationships in which there is a fair balance of giving and taking
Respect: to be respectful towards myself or others; to be polite, considerate and show positive regard
Responsibility: to be responsible and accountable for my actions
Romance: to be romantic; to display and express love or strong affection
Safety: to secure, protect, or ensure safety of myself or others
Self-awareness: to be aware of my own thoughts, feelings and actions
Self-care: to look after my health and wellbeing, and get my needs met
Self-development: to keep growing, advancing or improving in knowledge, skills, character, or life experience.
Self-control: to act in accordance with my own ideals
Sensuality: to create, explore and enjoy experiences that stimulate the five senses

Sexuality: to explore or express my sexuality

Spirituality: to connect with things bigger than myself

Stability: to prioritize a sense of balance, consistency, and predictability

Skillfulness: to continually practice and improve my skills, and apply myself fully when using them

Supportiveness: to be supportive, helpful, encouraging, and available to myself or others

Trust: to be trustworthy; to be loyal, faithful, sincere, and reliable

ENDNOTES

CHAPTER 1

1 Mishel, Lawrence, and Julia Wolfe. 2019. "CEO compensation has grown 940% since 1978." Economic Policy Institute. https://epi.org/171191.

2 Gelles, David. 2022. The Man Who Broke Capitalism: How Jack Welch Gutted the Heartland and Crushed the Soul of Corporate America—and How to Undo His Legacy. New York: Simon & Schuster.

3 PwC. Global M&A Industry Trends: 2022 Outlook. PwC, 2022.

4 Lev, Baruch. 2024. "We analyzed 40,000 M&A deals over 40 years. Here's why 70-75% fail." Fortune. https://fortune.com/2024/11/13/we-analyzed-40000-mergers-acquisitions-ma-deals-over-40-years-why-70-75-percent-fail-leadership-finance/.

5 Hyman, Louis. 2018. Temp: How American Work, American Business, and the American Dream Became Temporary. New York: Penguin Random House LLC.

6 Bureau of Labor Statistics, Workers' Expectations About Losing and Replacing Their Jobs: 35 Years of Change, citing General Social Survey data on job-loss expectations for 1982.

7 Gallup News Service. Despite Recent Wave of Corporate Layoffs, Most Americans Not Worried About Losing Their Job. Gallup, January 10–14, 2001.

8 2025 Jobs & Pay Report. Bankrate.com, 2025

9 Association for Talent Development. ASTD State of the Industry Report 2004. ASTD, 2004.

10 McKinsey & Company, referenced in Stéphane Garelli, "Why You Will Probably Live Longer Than Most Big Companies," IMD Business School (Dec. 2016), noting that the average life-span of companies listed in the S&P 500 has decreased substantially over decades.

11 Layoffs.fyi data reported in "There were more than 250,000 layoffs in the tech industry in 2023," Android Headlines, January 17, 2024

12 Lyons, Dan. 2016. Disrupted: My Misadventure in the Start-Up Bubble. New York: Hachette Books.

13 Small Business Administration, Office of Advocacy, Small Business Facts, "Survival Rates for Small Businesses" (data on employer establishment survival rates), accessed [date], https://sbecouncil.org/about-us/facts-and-data/

14 Yale Insights, "A Wave of Acquisitions May Have Shielded Big Tech from Competition", summarizing Ederer & Pellegrino's study using NVCA data, showing that VCbacked acquisitions rose from about 10 % to ~90 % of exits over the last ~30 years (1985–2019)

15 Top US-Based Tech Companies by Number of Employees. Accessed December 30, 2025. https://techbehemoths.com/blog/top-us-based-tech-companies-number-employees?utm_source=chatgpt.com

16 Higher Education Research Institute, The American Freshman: Twenty Year Trends, 1966–1985 (UCLA School of Education & Information Studies)

17 ASCD, "The Ambitious Generation,"

18 U.S. Bureau of Labor Statistics, Occupational Outlook Handbook: Physicians and Surgeons, showing that about 23,600 annual openings for physicians and surgeons are projected on average from 2024–34. U.S. Bureau of Labor Statistics. Accessed December 30, 2025. https://www.bls.gov/ooh/healthcare/physicians-and-surgeons.htm

19 Bureau of Labor Statistics. Unemployment in October 2009. The Economics Daily, November 10, 2009. https://www.bls.gov/opub/ted/2009/ted_20091110.htm

20 Pew Research Center. Cumulative Student Debt Among Recent College Graduates. October 7, 2014. https://www.pewresearch.org/social-trends/2014/10/07/cumulative-student-debt-among-recent-college-graduates/

21 Bersin & Associates, *The Corporate Learning Factbook* 2010: *Benchmarks, Trends and Analysis of the U.S. Training Market,* Available via PR Newswire, January 13, 2009. https://www.prnewswire.com/news-releases/bersin-associates-study-shows-significant-drop-in-employee-learning-and-development-spending-for-second-consecutive-year-81315497.html

22 RecruitiFi. Millennial Outlook Survey. RecruitiFi, July 21, 2015. https://www.prnewswire.com/news-releases/millennials-know-job-hopping-looks-bad-yet-86-would-not-think-twice-about-leaving-their-job-recruitifi-survey-finds-300116005.html

CHAPTER 2

23 Hewlett, Sylvia A., and C. B. Luce. 2006. "Extreme jobs: The dangerous allure of the 70-hour work week." Harvard Business Review 84, no. 12 (December): 49-59.

24 World Health Organization. 2019. "Burn-out an "occupational phenomenon": International Classification of Diseases." Burn-out an "occupational phenomenon": International Classification of Diseases. https://www.who.int/news/item/28-05-2019-burn-out-an-occupational-phenomenon-in-international-classification-of-diseases.

25 Nagoski, Emily, and Amelia Nagoski. 2019. Burnout: The Secret to Unlocking the Stress Cycle. New York City: Random House Publishing Group.

26 Curran, Thomas, and Andrew P. Hill. 2017. "Perfectionism Is Increasing Over Time: A Meta-Analysis of Birth Cohort Differences from 1989 to 2016." Psychological Bulletin 145, no. 4 (November): 410-429. https://doi.org/10.1037/bul0000138.

27 McKinsey and Company and Lean In. 2022. "Women in the Workplace 2022." https://womenintheworkplace.com/2022.

CHAPTER 3

28 Marcia, James E. "Development and Validation of Ego-Identity Status." *Journal of Personality and Social Psychology* 3, no. 5 (1966): 551–558

29 Kahneman, Daniel, and Amos Tversky. "Prospect Theory: An Analysis of Decision under Risk." Econometrica 47, no. 2 (1979): 263–291

30 Staw, Barry M. "Knee-Deep in the Big Muddy: A Study of Escalating Commitment to a Chosen Course of Action." Organizational Behavior and Human Performance 16, no. 1 (1976): 27–44. DOI: 10.1016/0030-5073(76)90005-2

31 Stamm, B. H. The Concise ProQOL Manual, 2nd Ed. Pocatello, ID: ProQOL.org, 2010.

32 Tversky, Amos, and Daniel Kahneman. "Judgment under Uncertainty: Heuristics and Biases." Science 185, no. 4157 (1974): 1124–31.

CHAPTER 4

33 *Startup Failure Statistics for Investors & Founders,* Seosandwitch (2025), noting that **90 % of startups ultimately fail** based on aggregated industry failure data.

34 Phenom, *Fortune* 500 *Study: Most Organizations Failing to Match Candidates with the Right Work Using Data and Context* (2024 State of Candidate Experience: 2024 Benchmarks Report), https://www.phenom.com/press-release/fortune-500-study-most-organizations-failing-to-match-candidates-with-the

35 Hogarth, Robin M., Tomás Lejarraga, and Emre Soyer. "The Two Settings of Kind and Wicked Learning Environments." Current Directions in Psychological Science 24, no. 5 (2015): 379–85.

CHAPTER 5

36 Brookings Institution. The history of women's work and wages and how it has created success for us all, Brookings (historical data on female labor force participation around 1900)

37 Historical Statistics of the United States, Colonial Times to 1970, Bicentennial Edition (Washington, D.C.: U.S. Census Bureau, 1975), www.nces.ed.gov/pubs2000/Digest99/d99t249.html

38 U.S. Department of Education, National Center for Education Statistics. Degree Attainment by Gender, 2022–23, as reported in "Men vs Women: Who Has More College Degrees?" Higher Ed Morning (2023)

39 Pew Research Center. For Women's History Month: A Look at Gender Gains and Gaps in the U.S., February 27, 2024

40 Women Business Collaborative, Women CEOs in America 2024 Executive Summary. https://wbcollaborative.org/.../2024-executive-summary/

41 McKinsey & Company, Women in the Workplace 2023–2025 Report (2024), https://www.mckinsey.com/.../women-in-the-workplace-report

42 Pew Research Center. Survey on Gender Obstacles and Perceptions of Sexism in the U.S. (2016)

43 Loden, Marilyn. Feminine Leadership: Or, How to Succeed in Business Without Being One of the Boys. New York: Berkley Books, 1985

44 McKinsey & Company and LeanIn.Org, Women in the Workplace 2022 (McKinsey & Company, 2022), https://mckinsey.com/~/media/mckinsey/featured%20insights/diversity%20and%20inclusion/women%20in%20the%20workplace%202022/women-in-the-workplace-2022.pdf

45 Ryan, Michelle K., and S. Alexander Haslam. The Glass Cliff: Evidence That Women Are OverRepresented in Precarious Leadership Positions. British Journal of Management 16, no. 2 (2005): 81–90

46 Zippia, Chief Diversity Officer Demographics and Statistics, showing that 54.5 % of chief diversity officers are women (2025). https://www.zippia.com/chief-diversity-officer-jobs/demographics/

47 ive Mint, "The Rise and Fall of the Chief Diversity Officer," (2023). https://www.livemint.com/companies/the-rise-and-fall-of-the-chief-diversity-officer-11689940865230.html

48 National Research Council. The Maternal Wall: Research and Discrimination Against Mothers. Washington, DC: National Academies Press.

49 Miller, Claire Cain. "A Child Helps Your Career, if You're a Man: The Motherhood Penalty vs. the Fatherhood Bonus." The New York Times, September 6, 2014. https://www.nytimes.com/2014/09/07/upshot/a-child-helps-your-career-if-youre-a-man.htm

50 Press Association, The Guardian, August 11, 2014 https://www.theguardian.com/money/2014/aug/12/managers-avoid-hiring-younger-women-maternity-leave

51 Bachen, Christine M., Robert McLoughlin, and Carla G. Garcia. "What's in a Name: Exposing Gender Bias in Student Ratings of Teaching." Innovative Higher Education 39, no. 1 (2014): https://doi.org/10.1007/s1075501493134

52 Snyder, Kieran (2014). Gender bias in performance reviews: Reported summary in Fortune and HR publications.

SECTION 2

53 Quoidbach J, Gilbert DT, Wilson TD. The end of history illusion. Science 339, no 6115. 2013 Jan 4: 96-98

54 Navalent CEO Genome Project (as summarized in ghSMART), When Getting Fired Is Good for Your Career, October 31, 2018 https://ghsmart.com/insights/when-getting-fired-is-good-for-your-career/

CHAPTER 7

55 Anderson et al., A TwoFactor Scale of Perceived Power

CHAPTER 9

56 David, Susan. 2016. Emotional Agility: Get Unstuck, Embrace Change, and Thrive in Work and Life. New York: Penguin Publishing Group.

CHAPTER 10

57 The Sponsor Effect: Breaking Through the Last Glass Ceiling," Harvard Business Review

58 "Same, Same but Different? A Comparative Study of Women's Networking for Career Success in Germany and India." Asia Pacific Journal of Management (2025). https://doi.org/10.1007/s10490-025-10099-1

59 Katherine W. Phillips, Katie A. Liljenquist, and Margaret A. Neale, "Better Decisions Through Diversity," Insight (Kellogg School of Management, October 1, 2010), Kellogg Insight

60 Fishbach, Ayelet & Eyal, Tal & Finkelstein, Stacey. (2010). How Positive and Negative Feedback Motivate Goal Pursuit. Social and Personality Psychology Compass. Ayelet Fishbach, Minjung Koo, Stacey R. Finkelstein, Chapter Five - Motivation Resulting from Completed and Missing Actions.Advances in Experimental Social Psychology, 2014, Pages 257-307

61 Ibarra, Herminia. 2004. Working Identity: Unconventional Strategies for Reinventing Your Career. Brighton: Harvard Business School Press.

CHAPTER 11

62 Jie Chen, Woon Sau Leung, Wei Song, Marc Goergen, Why female board representation matters: The role of female directors in reducing male CEO overconfidence, Journal of Empirical Finance, Volume 53, 2019

63 Patti J. Fisher, Ph.D. (Virginia Tech) and Rui Yao, Ph.D. (University of Missouri). "Gender Differences in Financial Risk Tolerance."

64 van den Bos R, Harteveld M, Stoop H. Stress and decision-making in humans: performance is related to cortisol reactivity, albeit differently in men and women. Psychoneuroendocrinology. 2009 Nov;34(10):1449-58. doi: 10.1016/j.psyneuen.2009.04.016. Epub 2009 Jun 3. PMID: 19497677.

65 Nave, Gideon and Nadler, Amos and Zava, David and Camerer, Colin. Single dose testosterone administration impairs cognitive reflection in men. Psychological Science, 2017

SECTION 3

66 Jesmine La Russa, "5 Strategic Signals That Indicate Your Company Needs Fractional Executive Leadership,"

LinkedIn (Sept. 9, 2025), https://www.linkedin.com/pulse/5-strategic-signals-indicate-your-company-needs-fractionalexecutiveleadershipjesminelarussa

67 World Economic Forum, Global Gender Gap Report 2022, https://www.weforum.org/publications/global-gender-gap-report2022/infull/23gendergapsinfoundingbusinesses/

CHAPTER 13

68 Zenger Folkman. Episode 23: Are Women Better Leaders Than Men? The 90th Percentile Podcast, January 31, 2023 https://zengerfolkman.com/episode-23-are-women-better-leaders-than-men-2/

CHAPTER 14

69 Shappley, Jennifer. LinkedIn (2022) https://www.linkedin.com/business/talent/blog/product-tips/linkedin-members-spotlight-career-breaks-on-profiles?utm_source=chatgpt.com

70 Bowen, Tom. Gusto (2024) https://gusto.com/resources/gusto-insights/workers-are-taking-more-sabbatical-time

71 "The Transformative Power of Sabbaticals." AOM Insights

72 https://www.myperfectresume.com/career-center/careers/basics/career-gaps

CHAPTER 15

73 World Economic Forum, "*Women entrepreneurship is soaring in the US, a new survey finds,*" July 2022 https://www.weforum.org/agenda/2022/07/women-entrepreneurs-gusto-gender/

74 Gusto. 2024 New Business Formation Report. April 2, 2024 https://gusto.com/resources/gusto-insights/new-business-formation-report-2024

75 ARCAP, Gender Report on VC DecisionMakers

76 TechCrunch, "WomenFounded Startups Raised 1.9% of All VC Funds in 2022, a Drop from 2021," January 18, 2023 https://techcrunch.com/2023/01/18/women-founded-startups-raised-1-9-of-all-vc-funds-in-2022adropfrom2021/

77 McKinsey & Company, Underestimated Startup Founders: The Untapped Opportunity (June 23, 2023) https://www.mckinsey.com/featuredinsights/diversityandinclusion/underestimatedstartupfounderstheuntappedopportunity

78 Pew Research Center, Americans See Men as Financial Providers Even as Women's Contributions Grow (September 20, 2017), https://www.pewresearch.org/shortreads/2017/09/20americansseemenasthefinancialprovidersevenaswomenscontributionsgrow/

79 Kellogg Insight. 2019. "How Old Are Successful Tech Entrepreneurs?" KelloggInsight. https://insight.kellogg.northwestern.edu/article/younger-older-tech-entrepreneurs.

80 Stripe, Startup statistics you should know (2025), https://stripe.com/resources/more/startup-statistics-you-should-know

www.ingramcontent.com/pod-product-compliance
Lightning Source LLC
LaVergne TN
LVHW010543160826
845677LV00013B/2979

* 9 7 9 8 9 9 5 4 4 7 3 0 6 *